Jean-Baptiste Morin

Astrologia Gallica
Book Twenty-Four
Progressions and Transits

Translated from the Latin

By

James Herschel Holden, M.A.

Fellow of the American Federation
of Astrologers

First Printing 2005

ISBN: 0-86690-520-0

Published by:
American Federation of Astrologers, Inc.
6535 S. Rural Road
Tempe, AZ 85283

Printed in the United States of America

This book is for Robert Corre,
who asked for it.

TABLE OF CONTENTS

Translator's Preface   vii

Book Twenty-Four

Section I. Progressions

Chapter 1. Why the Old Astrologers Introduced Progressions 1

Chapter 2. How Many Modes of Progressions have
been Invented   5

Chapter 3. The Annual, Monthly, and Daily Progressions of
the Old [Astrologers] are Mere Figments of the Imagination   8

Section II. The Transits and Syzygies of the Planets

Chapter 1. How Should the Doctrine of Transits be Made   21

Chapter 2. What Path Previous Astrologers Followed
in Taking Notice of the Virtue of the Stars   22

Chapter 3. Whether the Transits of All the Planets Through
the Individual Places of the Nativity Should be Observed   26

Chapter 4. Whether in an Individual House of the
Nativity any Force Exceeds [that of] the Natal Chart
for Future Accidents of Life   28

Chapter 5. Whether all the Transits Through the Places of
the Nativity are Effective, or Whether They Alone and
in Some Way Motivate our own Nature to the Effects   36

Chapter 6. Whether the Transiting Planets Determine
the Places of their own Transits, or Whether They are
Determined by Them, and in what Way   39

Chapter 7. Whether the Transits of the Planets through
the Places of the Revolutions should be Looked at   40

Chapter 8. Whether for the Production of all the Effects
Happening to Men, the Transits Agreeing with their

Directions and Revolutions are Necessary, and at what Time 41

Chapter 9. For a Given Direction Presaging a Significant Event, which Planet's Transit is more Necessary for the Production of the Effect, and through which Place, so that the Transit may be Said to be Concordant 43

Chapter 10. In which by many Examples and Observations the Virtue of Transits and their Actual Efficacy are Confirmed 48

Chapter 11. [Determining] the Exact time of Events by a Transit, and Whether their Latitude should be Observed. The Doctrine Confirmed by Celestial Charts 57

Chapter 12. Whether the Planets act upon the Native through their own Syzygies Outside of the Places of the Nativity through which their Transits are Customarily Made. And How and When 46

Chapter 13. The Aphorisms or Principal Laws of Transits 72

Chapter 14. How from What has been Explained so far, Events of the Future can be Predicted by the Stars with Regard to the Kind [of Event], the Year, the Day, and the Hour 78

Chapter 15. Some Principal Rules of Prudence to be [Observed] by an Astrologer in Bringing Forth a Useful Opinion from the Stars 89

Appendix 1. The Equation of Time 103

Index of Persons 105

Bibliography 108

Translator's Preface

Morin's method of making predictions of events in the life of a particular individual is set forth in the main in four books of the *Astrologia Gallica*, namely Book 21 on Determinations,[1] Book 22 on Primary Directions,[2] Book 23 on Revolutions,[3] and Book 24 on Progressions and Transits. To understand the method fully, it is necessary to read all four books, preferably in sequence.

The present Book 24 on Progressions and Transits follows naturally after Book 23 on Revolutions, since Morin says there that transits can be used in connection with solar and lunar revolutions (or *returns*, as they are called nowadays) to determine the exact day on which a predicted event will occur.

However, he begins Book 24 with a lengthy diatribe against what he calls "progressions," by which he means both methods using equal degrees for years or months and methods using the elaborate systems set forth by the Arabian astrologers, some of which, unbeknownst to him, had been taken from Greek astrology books that were written during the classical period. These systems are properly called *profections*, but that term has fallen into disuse among modern astrologers, and they are now usually termed *symbolic progressions*. The more common ones in use today are the

---

[1] *The Morinus System of Astrological Interpretation...Astrologia Gallica/Book Twenty One* (Washington, D.C.: A.F.A., Inc. 1974). Still available.

[2] *Astrologia Gallica/Book Twenty-Two/Directions* (Tempe, Az.: A.F.A., Inc., 1994).

[3] *Astrologia Gallica/Book Twenty-Three/Revolutions* (Tempe, Az.: A.F.A., Inc., 2002).

radix system[4] and the so-called *solar arc*[5]. Aside from these, there is a little-used system of symbolic progressions called *tertiary progressions*.

Morin's complaint against all of the profections is that they are not based on anything astronomical—what he calls "true motion." He does not mention Placidus's Secondary Directions, which had perhaps not come to his attention, since Morin died only a few years after Placidus's books were published. His general complaint against symbolic directions would not have been applicable to secondaries, since they do depend upon "true motions."

Having stated at length his objections to symbolic directions, Morin sets forth his doctrine of how life events—*accidents*, to use the technical term—occur and how they can be predicted. Minor events can sometimes result from transits alone; but in general, Morin says that to attempt to predict important events in a native's life that happen at specific times we must consider several things. The first of these is the nativity itself, which predicts in a general way everything that will happen to the Native, the second is its primary directions, the third is the solar and lunar revolutions and their directions, and the fourth is the transits. We may perhaps illustrate Morin's explanation of how transits operate by offering an analogy. The nativity is like a gun of a certain type and caliber. The directions and revolutions are like shells of a particular type, and the transits are like the *trigger* of the gun.

For an event of a particular type to happen in the life of a native, it must first be indicated in his nativity. Next, it must be made

---

[4] A "degree for a year" method (actually employing the Naibod measure of $0°59'08''$ per year), admirably set forth in the book by Vivian Robson, *The Radix System* (London: The Stallex Publishing Co., 1930). It also expounds "tertiary directions."

[5] Those who use the "solar arc" might assert that it does actually represent the tone motion of the Sun. And that is true, but applying it to the motion of everything else in the natal chart is not valid from Morin's point of view, because it is only "true motion" for the Sun, not for anything else in the chart.

possible by a concordant primary direction, which establishes the time within plus or minus a year when an event of that type can happen. But without a concordant solar revolution in one of those years, the event still cannot happen (or at least only in a very minor way). More strength is given to the manifestation of the event by primary directions of the annual revolution and by a concordant lunar revolution. But the final impetus is from a concordant transit. By analogy then, the general nature of the event is one that could result from a gun of a certain type and caliber, the possibility of the occurrence of the event is the loading of a particular type of shell into the gun, and the actual manifestation of the event is accomplished by pulling the trigger.

Thus, we can see why a certain type of direction or revolution or transit may occur many times in a particular chart without producing any noticeable effect. For an effect to occur, there must be a complete combination of concordant factors. To return to the analogy of the gun, if we wanted to kill a large animal, we must have a large caliber gun, and it must be loaded with a heavy caliber shell, and we must aim the gun precisely, and pull the trigger. If any one of these actions is not taken, then we will not bring down the elephant. Obviously, pulling the trigger on an unloaded gun will accomplish nothing. And this is why a particular transit may occur numerous times without any noticeable result, but now and then it does produce a result. And looked at from the other direction, in order for a certain event to occur in the life of a Native, that event must first be signified in his nativity. Again by analogy, we cannot bring down an elephant by firing a B-B gun at it, nor by pulling the trigger on a gun of whatever caliber loaded with blanks. The former case corresponds to a weak nativity and the latter to a nativity with no operative direction and a concordant revolution.

But this is enough to give the Reader the basic idea of Morin's doctrine. To understand it fully, he must read the text attentively and think about what he has read. Morin illustrates the procedure with actual example charts set for the time of significant events in the lives of several persons. These deserve close scrutiny.

I should mention that Book 24, Section II, Chapters 12-14 were translated previously and published in the Addenda to my translation of Book 22. But I have revised the earlier translation for the present work.

The translation itself is fairly literal, but it is less elegant than Morin's Latin, which has a very extensive vocabulary that I have not tried to emulate by using uncommon English words. I do waver between referring to a planet as "it" and as "he" or "she." I have done this to make the referents as specific in English as they are in the Latin. And I have preserved some of Morin's astrological terms that are now obsolescent, such as "accident," "figure," "nativity," "virtue," "revolution," "syzygy," "constitution," etc. Those who have read my translations of Books 22 and 23 will be familiar with these. I do not use the term "horoscope" because Morin uses the Latin word *horoscopus* only in its original sense of "ascendant," which I translate uniformly as "ASC." Instead, I translate *nativitas* as "nativity," and another term that he uses, *genesis*, sometimes as "chart" and sometimes as "nativity." I do not believe that he intended to make a distinction between *nativitas* and *genesis*, but he merely used them as synonyms to avoid the constant repetition of the same word. It would have been appropriate to have translated another frequent synonym *figura* as "chart," but since this is after all a 17th century work, I thought it better to render it simply as "figure." The word *locus* usually means "place," which can be a house or the cusp of a house, a planet, the aspect of a planet, or the Part of Fortune. In this book, since he is frequently referring to transits, revolutions, and directions that share some similarity and thus *coordinate* to indicate the same event, he often uses the Latin word *congruus* 'agreeable' to indicate that similarity. In my translation of Book 23, I sometimes translated it as 'conformable' and sometimes as 'concordant'; here, I have usually translated it as 'concordant'. And of course I have kept the frequently used word *Caelum* as a technical term rather than translate it as "sky," and I have also retained *Primum Mobile* in its Latin form.

I might also mention that in my translation of Book 22 I translated the word *morbus* as "sickness," but in my translation of Book 23 and also here I have translated it as "illness." In American English "sickness" and "illness" are more or less interchangeable, although "illness" is perhaps more formal and consequently less often used. But in British English "sickness" more often refers to indigestion, while "illness" is the generic term.

Furthermore, Morin's printed text often uses the astrological symbols for the planets, signs, and the Part of Fortune, and sometimes uses them for the aspects. I have not done this; instead, I have spelled out their names.

Finally, the Reader who takes up this book without having read the translations of books 21, 22, and 23, will no doubt find it hard reading. He may then wonder if the translation was properly done. I can assure him that the Latin text is more difficult to read than the translation and that without resorting to unlicensed paraphrase it would be difficult to render it into easy English. Morin had a thorough command of Latin and had learned to write what are called "periodic sentences." These are sentences that go on and on with a dozen or more clauses. (Those who have struggled to decipher Cicero's speeches to the Senate in Third Year Latin will know what I mean.) I have occasionally broken those monsters into two or more parts, but usually I have kept them together with a liberal use of commas, semi-colons and dashes. I have also added words in brackets here and there and even added some explanatory footnotes to make the translation more understandable. Still, it is not easy to read, and the Reader who wants to understand what Morin was trying to impart to him will from time to time find some sentences that he will have to re-read and think about. I believe that if he does that he will understand them, and he will be glad that he took the trouble to do so.

As practical examples, Morin inserts several charts in this book that are set for the time at which an important accident occurred in the life of a native. In the associated discussion, reference is made to the natal horoscope and to solar or lunar revolutions (returns), but those charts are not given, since Morin had included them in earlier books of the *Astrologia Gallica*. Most of them are shown in my translation of Book 23, so I did not think it necessary to repeat them here.

The charts in this translation are facsimiles of the charts in the *Astrologia Gallica* and are therefore in the old square form. The Reader should note that in the center of the charts the day of the month and the time in hours are given, both reckoned from the preceding noon. I have given the date and time reckoned from the previous midnight below each chart. The times are all stated in Local Apparent Time. If the Reader wishes to recalculate the charts with a modern computer, he must first convert the time in LAT to the equivalent time in Local Mean Time. This can easily be done by reference to the Equation of Time table in Appendix 1.

Finally, I would like to emphasize what I said at the beginning of this Preface: Morin's complete method of prediction is set forth in Books 21-24 of the *Astrologia Gallica*. The Reader who tries to learn it by reading only one or two of those books will not acquire the whole method but only pieces of it. The method itself is straightforward in theory but complicated in details. Admittedly, reading four books to learn how to predict one event seems to be both daunting and excessive. But the diligent Reader's patience will be rewarded.

James H. Holden
September 2002

ASTROLOGIA GALLICA

BOOK TWENTY-FOUR
PROGRESSIONS & TRANSITS

PREFACE

The doctrine of annual, monthly, and daily Progressions of the significators of a Nativity handed down by Ptolemy in the last chapter of the Quadripartite *and by his commentator Cardan and approved by all others we have dismissed in the* Rudolphine Tables *that we have abbreviated, treating of the Revolutions of the Sun & the Moon, whose directions we have said should be adopted in place of progressions. And although we have not set forth there all the reasons for this sort of a change, still we have said a few things; for in fact they have seemed to be reasonable and pleasing to the superior astrologers, so that without controversy they are received by them. But in this Book and in Book 23, which is on those same Revolutions and their directions, the whole matter is [made] very clear & manifest by reasons and experiences, so that there would seem to be no topic of it remaining in ambiguity, but that which pertains to the transits of the planets over the places of the Nativity and the Revolutions, which the Old Astrologers were accustomed to [consider] to be divisors of times of small virtue. But that there is certainly inherent in them not a small but a very great force with regard to the Sublunar things that they particularly affect, we not only declare, but we also prove with valid reasons and experiences. Which surely will compel every Reader, studious in Astrology, to acknowledge, to whom the nature of the celestial light shall have bestowed something in his own nativity.*

SECTION I.
Progressions.

Chapter 1.
Why the Old Astrologers Introduced Progressions.

Since Ptolemy and the other Old Astrologers directed only five *significators* for the life of the native and all of his accidents, namely the ASC, the MC, the Sun, the Moon, and the Part of Fortune, having omitted Saturn, Jupiter, Mars, Venus, [and] Mercury, and [those] were not sufficient for them, they thought that the number of *promissors*, which they wished to be dividers of the entire time of life of the native, ought to be multiplied. Therefore, to the bodies of the 7 planets & their aspects, they adjoined 60 other promissors and of course the 5 *terms* of each sign assigned to those same Saturn, Mars, Jupiter Venus [and] Mercury,[1] the worthlessness of which we have revealed elsewhere.[2] And so, from an excess of promissors, compensating for a deficiency of significators, to bring about, that in no year might anything significant happen that could not be said to have been caused by some radical direction, whether truly or falsely.

But actually, because it is not sufficient to foresee and predict the year of an accident, but the knowledge of the day of that accident is particularly required, lest, from blind uncertainty the native should be concerned about that in vain throughout an entire year, and because to the Old [Astrologers] there were lacking [any] ways by means of which they might arrive at that mystery, they introduced *progressions* for the minute division of time through equal degrees, about which Ptolemy treats in the last chapter of Book 4 of the *Quadripartite*,[3] expounding the force for their use

---

[1] Reading ♃ ♀ ☿ instead of ♃ and ☿.

[2] See Book 15, Chapter 13, on the various subdivisions of the signs (translated on pp. 237-240 of the Addenda to my translation of AG Book 22).

[3] In Robbins's ed. (Loeb Classical Library, 1940), *Tetrabiblos*, iv. 10 "Of the Di-

to determine the days of the effects. Therefore, this is the scheme of the introduction of progressions or processes.[4] Moreover, Cardan in his *Commentary*[5] has only two schemes, with which he commends Ptolemy's doctrine in this part. The first is "that it should be judged that he had accepted this opinion from the Egyptians, and the outstanding prophecies of Thrasybulus about Tiberius, of Sulla, his son, about Nero and Caligula, of Ascletarion about Domitian and himself.[6] Since Ptolemy himself was a very diligent and reliable man; and if [those things] were noted, it is hardly to be doubted that he had followed their path and handed them down."[7]

But to this I reply: That Ptolemy, Book 1, Chapter 9, had re-

---

vision of Times," in which Ptolemy first defines the planetary rulerships of the ages of man (called by the Arabs *alfridaries*), giving in order: age 1-4 to the Moon, 5-14 to Mercury, 15-22 to Venus, 23-37 to Mars, 38-56 to the Sun, 57-68 to Jupiter, and 69 until the end of life to Saturn. Next he applies what amounts to zodiacal primary directions to the ASC degree, the Part of Fortune, the Moon, the Sun, and the MC; and he calls these "general chronocrators." Then he mentions the "annual chronocrators," which are formed by allowing one year to a sign, the "monthly chronocrators," allowing one sign to each space of 28 days, and the diurnal chronocrators allowing 2⅓ days to a sign. And finally, he speaks of the transits of the planets.

[4] I take the Latin word *processus* 'advances' to be what are properly called 'profections', but which nowadays are usually called 'symbolic progressions'.

[5] Jerome Cardan, *Claudii Ptolemaei Pelusiensis Libri quatuor De Astrorum Iudiciis cum expositione Hieronymi Cardani, Opera omnia* (Lyons: Hugnetan & Ravaud, 1663.10 vols.), vol. 5, pp. 93-368.

[6] The astrologers mentioned by Cardan were in fact Tiberius Claudius Thrasyllus (d. 36), his son Tiberius Claudius Balbillus (d.c.81), Sulla (mentioned by Suetonius in his life of Caligula but quite possibly a mistake for Balbillus), and Asclation (rather than Ascletarion), who was ordered by Domitian to be executed the day before the latter's predicted murder on 18 September 96. See Frederick H. Cramer, *Astrology in Roman Law and Politics* (Philadelphia: The American Philosophical Society, 1954).

[7] Jerome Cardan, loc. cit, p.363, col. 2. Morin cuts short the last sentence, which reads in full "...it is hardly to be doubted that *it was necessary that* he follow their path, *which had been confirmed by evident predictions*," (Words omitted by Morin in italics.)

jected the doctrine of the Egyptians concerning the terms and had embraced the Chaldean [doctrine],[8] even though both are worthless, as we have shown in its own place. And at the end of the chapter, he also rejects many other divisions of the signs handed down by those oriental peoples because they were lacking any physical reason (he says, but) devised for pretence; therefore, we also are permitted to reject the doctrine of progressions, if they do not repose upon a physical reason, and since Ptolemy has no reason for it, he was equally able to reject that as well as the doctrine of those same Egyptians about the terms, and their other figments, but which one looks at for those prophecies of the ancients, then [those] of the more recent men, Francesco Maria of Ferrara[9] and Paris Ceresara[10] of Mantua; Cardan proves that they had predicted the days of the events by equal progressions alone,[11] and that no other way of predicting was known to those astrologers, since they handed down their own methods of predicting to their successors

---

[8] Not true! Ptolemy, *Tetrabiblos* i. 20 & 21, does complain that the Terms According to the Egyptians lack any obvious rationale, and he says that the schematic version of the Terms According to the Chaldeans is simpler, but he also says ate that, "Now of these terms, those which are constituted by the Egyptian method are, as we said, more worthy of credence, both because in the form in which they have been collected by the Egyptian writers they have for their utility been deemed worthy of record, and because for the most part the degrees of these terms are consistent with the nativities which have been recorded by them as examples." (Robbins's translation)

[9] Francesco Maria was said by Count Henry von Rantzau (1526-1598) to have predicted the year, day, and hour of his death to Jacopo Piccinino [1420-1465] (see Lynn Thomdike, *History of Magic and Experimental Science* (New York: Columbia University Press, 1923-1958. 8 vols.), vol. 6,136. Hereinafter cited as HMES.

[10] Paris Ceresara (c. 1466-1532), a jurisconsult and astrologer of Mantua, who was said by both Stadius (c. 1550-1593) and Tucci to have predicted Cardinal Alessandro Farnese's accession to the papal throne (he became Paul III); and Pontus de Tyard (1521-1605) relates that Ceresara had made the prediction 12 years before the event, also that he would be in peril of drowning in seven years, and that he would die after twenty-seven years [which in fact happened, since he acceded to the throne in 1534 and died in 1559] (see Thorndike, HMES 5,256).

[11] Jerome Cardan, *De Revolutions Annorum, Mensium, et dierum...*, Chapter 12, loc. cit, p. 572, col. 2.

and did not illustrate it with examples.

The second scheme of Cardan's is "That everything that is done here depends on the motion and constitution of the heavens; and that everything that is seen to be unequal in the sky is referred to equality. Therefore, since a revolution of the Sun is unequal, the outcome of things in [those] years cannot be referred to it, but [rather] to the direction and profections through the signs."[12]

And yet I reply: Cardan is greatly deceived when he thinks that the occurrence of things is not from the unequal motion of the Sun and the Planets, which appears in the sky, and is true and real, but is from their equal motion, which is only fictitious[13] and in the intellect, but not in the [real] nature of things, since the equal motion of the planets was only devised with this end and reduced into tables, so that from it as an intermediary and from the equations of the center, their true place may be known, from which alone there are sublunar effects.

Chapter 2.
How many Modes of Progressions have been Invented.

Progressions were only devised for one purpose, that with their help the days of accidents might be determined. Moreover, when the human intellect, having forsaken the light of reason, loosens the reins to [accept] fictions, it is marvelous how much it runs riot in these, as is apparent in this doctrine of progressions, in which, for finding the day of the very same accident, progressions

---

[12] Jerome Cardan, *Claudii Ptolemaei Pelusiensis...*, op. cit., p. 366. cols. 1&2. This confusing statement means that "equal" motions (such as *profections*) should be used for prediction; consequently, solar revolutions, which are irregular, cannot be used. Morin contradicts this statement in the next paragraph. And Cardan himself used both *profections* and solar revolutions, i.e. both "equal" and "unequal" motions.

[13] The Latin text has *fu/itius,* where the letter represented by / is uncertain. But I have conjectured that the word is mispelled and should be *fictitius* 'fictitious'.

of a threefold sort have been devised—that is, annual, monthly, and diurnal—some faster than others, lest of course, the day of the occurrence eluding one sort, might not evade another; moreover, there are some progressions (as they will have it) [that are] perambulations of the houses of the nativity, by which significators are conceived to be brought under the Zodiac according to the succession of the signs. For in fact the *Caelum* with respect to the natal scheme must be looked at in a threefold mode. First indeed, that it is disposed in the natal scheme itself; and so it should remain immobile. Second, that it is indeed also disposed in that same mode; but afterwards it is moved by directions and those progressions above the immobile natal scheme. And finally, third according as both the *Caelum* and the planets, by their ordinary motion, are in fact naturally carried by their own and their common [motion], they pass through the *Caelum* observed in the first and second mode. Furthermore, by direction, they are made [to move] in the first motion about the poles of the Equator, which is a real motion, and a true one, as we have said in Book 22. Progressions, however, are conceived to be made by equal motion about the poles of the Ecliptic, but they are not made by any true or real motion certainly, because no *Caelum* and no Planet moves by such a motion, as will be made plain below.

If in fact the annual progression is a motion by which a particular significator runs through precisely 30 degrees of the Zodiac with equal motion in each year, as if [for example] in the hour of a nativity the ASC was in 7°15′ of Aries; [then] at the beginning of the second year, that ASC by this progression was in 7°15′ of Taurus, and so on. Consequently, by this progression, any significator in a single day runs through 4′56″ or 296″ of the Ecliptic, by which measure it can be known from a table constructed for this [measure] in what place in the Ecliptic the significator is situated on the individual days of the year by this progression.

Moreover, the monthly progression or profection is a much swifter motion. In fact, they want to divide the tropical solar year

6

into 13 equal parts, which they call *profectional months*, each of which contains 28 days 2 hours 17 minutes; and they say that the significator of the first of these months runs through the first sign of the profection of the year, the second goes through the next sign, and so on, consequently running through 13 signs during the solar year; and hence it comes about that the significators produced by the annual and monthly progression, begin and end individual years with the same point of the *Caelum* in both progressions. Moreover, the significator runs through 1°04'04" per day by this motion, and there is also a table available for this use, as mentioned above.

Finally, the diurnal progression is the swiftest of all; namely, the one in which the monthly profection is again divided into 13 equal parts, which are called *profectional days*, each of which contains approximately 51 hours 52 minutes, for which there is also a table. And the first significator (as they will have it) of these days from the moment of the nativity, or of the revolution, runs through the sign of the first profectional month, the second day, the sign of the second month, and so forth. Whence it results, that in the beginnings of the individual profectional months there is the same point of the *Caelum* for the monthly profection and for its diurnal significator, which by this motion runs through the individual days in 13°52'52", for which there is also a table.

Next, we would have put here tables of the motion and the use of them, so that it might be known on what day any particular significator would come to any promissor by the annual, diurnal, or monthly progression; or vice versa, it might be deduced to which promissor any particular significator would come on an entered day. But this is available here and there in [the works of] Regiomontanus, Schoener, Junctinus, Origanus, and other astrologers. Besides, moreover, we have undertaken to show that those progressions are a vain figment [of the imagination], from which it seems to me that the Student of Astrology should be diverted, rather than being instructed in that with a major loss of my time.

Chapter 3.
The Annual, Monthly, and Daily Progressions of the Old [Astrologers] are Mere Figments of the Imagination.

Besides, there will be real motions common to the *Caelum* and the individual Planets, seeing that they want the cusps of the figure and the individual Planets to be progressed [as] significators with such motions; but neither the *Caelum*, nor the Sun, nor the Moon, nor the other Planets are borne as a matter of fact by such equal motions, as is known to all astronomers, and as can be proved by observations. For the *Primum Caelum* is not moved above the poles of the Ecliptic in the succession of the signs. And although the sphere of the fixed stars is moved thus, nevertheless it does not communicate its motion to the *Primum Caelum*, so that the ASC, the MC, and the places of the Planets seen in the *Primum Caelum*, are borne by that same motion. The sphere of the fixed stars is moved forward by its own motion in the order of the signs by only one degree in about 71 years—in truth, slower than the annual progression, [which] of course runs through 30 degrees in a single year. But as for the Planets, these in fact are moved over the poles of the Ecliptic, but all of them unequally with respect to us on account of their eccentricities and the inclinations of their orbits to the Equator; therefore, the progressions of the Old [Astrologers] are simply a pure figment of the imagination.

Cardan doggedly tried to defend this doctrine of Ptolemy in his own manner and to commend those progressions just like in the arena with three schemes, the first two of which we have refuted in Chapter 1, but the third one is this in Text 85, "That the annual progression agrees with the motion of the Sun and the motion of Jupiter, and the monthly one with the revolution of the Moon; and finally, the diurnal one with the space [of time] which the Moon spends in one sign."[14]

---

[14] Cardan, loc. Cit, p. 364, col. 2. = *Tetrabiblos*, iv. 10 (Robbins's translation, p. 455, lines 5-11).

Truly, he is dreaming and confused. For the time of the annual progression, that is a year, he assimilates to the period of the motion of the Sun or to the time in which Jupiter stays in a single sign. And yet, neither does Jupiter run precisely through one sign in a solar year, nor is it put in charge by nature of measuring a year, nor does the Sun run through a single sign during its period. And besides, while the annual period is for this reason assimilated to the whole period of the Sun, but thence to the twelfth part of Jupiter's period (which is no small confusion), it is left uncertain whether such a progression takes its powers of acting from the Sun or from Jupiter[15] or from both; therefore, the reasons in this part of Cardan's [book] are groundless.

Similarly, the profectional month of 28 days 2 hours and 17 minutes is compared to the lunar revolution; and he says that that month is intermediate between the periodic month of the Moon of 27 days and 8 hours and the synodic month of 29 days and 12 hours. But this is false, for the average of these is 28 days and 10 hours, not indeed 28 days 2 hours and 17 minutes, as Cardan had put it.

Finally, he compares the profectional day of 51 hours and 52 minutes with the space of time in which the Moon remains in one sign, when, nevertheless, this is several hours greater, whether you consider the Moon in the synodic month or in the periodic one.

Someone may say that amongst these progressions and the actual times of the motions of the planets mentioned above, there is no very great difference; and consequently they can be admitted. But truly, which motion is more like the true motion of the Sun either in its place or its time than its mean motion that is given in all the tables and is plainly fictitious? And yet no one has said that the actual effects of the Sun are from its mean motion, which has no other force aside from an intellectual one, but only for calculation,

---

[15] Reading *à Iove* 'from Jupiter' rather than *à vigesima quinta* 'from the twenty-fifth'.

for finding the true motion of the Sun from which are the actual effects. Finally, the question is not whether the progressions have an affinity with the times of the motion of the Sun, Jupiter, or the Moon, but whether any significators, that is the *Primum Caelum* and the Planets are truly and actually moved by these even motions of the progressions above the poles of the ecliptic, because no one of sound mind has said so. Therefore, one may say that it is necessary that such motions should only be fictitiously attributed to those significators; and consequently, from such a fictitious motion, only fictitious effects and not any real effects can arise. They are, therefore, only games of subtle imagination [played] in numbers without any logical reason for [the purpose of] show, as Ptolemy was saying above about those figments of the Egyptians and the Chaldeans; accordingly, it must be cast out from true Astrology. And the subtlety in it is that they provided so ingeniously that in each year from the beginning of the annual revolution, they have made the annual progression, the monthly and the daily progression, begin from the same point in the zodiac. I hesitate to say how ridiculous it is to suppose that any significator of the natal chart progresses by a fourfold motion in that chart, namely, by the motion of a radical direction, and then by an annual, monthly, and daily progression!

One can inquire further why in progressions equal times are measured by equal arcs of the ecliptic, but in directions by unequal arcs of time, since there ought to be a uniform measure of time, and the equator alone is a true, simple, uniform, and natural measure of time? And then, why is the latitude of the Planets taken into account in directions, but not in progressions? But neither to these [questions] nor to many others will anyone return any facts concordant with reason.

And no one should criticize us for determining the precise times of effects within a year by having introduced in place of progressions the annual and monthly directions of the revolutions. For we have done that because it seemed to us particularly absurd to assign fictitious causes to real effects. Therefore, we have tried with truly arduous labor to discover the true and natural causes, which would not only depend upon real fundamentals, but would also correspond to experience. Which we have proved how truly it was prescribed by us by numerous examples and calculations in Book 23; and all posterity will experience it with a grateful mind. Moreover, that it is shown in Book 23, Chapter 15, that the annual and monthly directions that have been adopted by us as real motions are none other than radical, and in truth a measure of time discovered by reason, is proved by experience in the aforesaid examples; and all this is confirmed by the uniformity of action of the celestial bodies through the figures and the directions subordinate to them, by which from universals to particulars, both the kind of effects as well as their time is arrived at.

Perhaps it might be said that the annual directions had already been used by the Old [Astrologers], as we have noted from Cardan at the beginning of Book 23, Chapter 15. And then the revolutions of the Moon adopted by us, as is set forth by that same Cardan in his *Book of Revolutions*, Chapter 13, when he says: "The Lights return to their own places in their revolutions."[16] Consequently, we cannot introduce anything new here for us to take pride in.

But I reply first that Cardan in his *Book of Revolutions*, Chapter 13, rejects the annual directions of the Old [Astrologers], and he has not disclosed their error, nor has he thought up any remedy for it, but we have provided both in [our] Book 23, Chapter 15.

I reply second that Cardan in Chapter 12 did indeed speak about the return of the Moon to her radical place in the monthly revolutions, but he neglected these revolutions [which] had not been well scrutinized, then because in that same place, doubting

---

[16] Rather, in Rule 4 of Chapter 11 (loc. cit, p. 570, col. 1), which reads "from this it may be inferred that only the Sun never forgets his entire disposition, similarly the Moon, where her return is made from the nativity. Moreover, this is especially done when the Sun or the Moon have returned to the same place in which they were in the nativity, for here in the lights it is the return to their own place, if the Moon is considered, in this manner."

their virtue, he says "where the monthly returns are made from the nativity," and a little later "if the Moon is considered in this manner," then because in Chapter 13 he sets forth and approves other revolutions of the Moon, which we have rejected from right causes in Book 23, Chapter 15. Add [the fact] that no one before us has propounded directions in the monthly revolution nor the measure of time for those same directions; whence, their truth has until now remained hidden and neglected; and we have not done this so that we might take pride in it, but so that we might serve the truth and give back the glory to God.

It will seem to be much more difficult to suppress those who assert that annual, monthly, and daily progressions are indeed confirmed by the frequent experiences of Astrologers, so that it becomes rash to reject them, and [it is] no light symbol of foolishness or ignorance, especially because they are expounded by Ptolemy and very much esteemed by his commentator Cardan, who has philosophized about Astrology more than all the other [Astrologers], and he makes use of them from time to time in his judgments of years.

But I reply. It can be objected similarly that no less frequent experiences of Astrologers with the terms of the Planets set forth by Ptolemy, which we have shown in Book 15, Chapter 13, to be the most groundless figment [of the imagination]. With regard to these things about the judgments of years, Cardan is not consistent. For in his *Book on the Judgments of Nativities*, Chapter 6,[17] he judges on his own accidents of the year from just the figure of the revolution, without any directions or progressions. But in his *Book of Nativities* at the end of the *Quadripartite*,[18] he judges on the years 53, 54-55, & 56 of his own nativity only from the directions and progressions, and the ingresses, i.e. the places of the Planets at the beginning of the solar revolution, without any regard to the fig-

---

[17] Chapter 6 "The Things signified by Revolutions and the Method of Judging them According to our own Opinion," loc. cit, pp. 440-443 (1662 ed.)

[18] I have not found these charts in vol. 5 of the 1662 edition.

ure of the revolution because elsewhere he forbade it—so badly is he inconsistent. and so groundless and ridiculous does he render Astrology, when he professes to be using it so indifferently. Then, in the second nativity at the end of the *Quadripartite*,[19] he even wants to refer these annual progressions only to the places of the nativity; and yet he confesses that he is uncertain about the monthly and daily ones, whether they should be referred to the places of the radix or to [those of] the annual revolution. Because Cardan argues doubtfully on their use, he only observed a coincidental truth. But since at the end of the judgment of his own nativity, he puts down that there happened to himself an accident involving an unexpected and painful illness in the year 1553 on the 20th of November at 2:30 PM, for which moment he erects a figure; and [since] he does not prescribe the day of anything else of this sort, it seems good to subject his judgment about that accident to an examination here.

First, he says that he had previously written that in that year he would enjoy good health, and so he had been a false prophet to himself, which in fact I marvel at. For the Sun in the sixth house of the nativity and even the Moon in the twelfth house, are significators of illnesses; moreover, the Sun in that year is directed to the 22nd degree of Sagittarius opposite Saturn, according to Cardan, but not to 18°51′, as he badly calculated. Besides, in the revolution for that year, erected by us and placed here, Mercury and the Moon are the rulers of the eighth; Mercury, moreover, is in the twelfth and in the watery sign of Mars, moreover the Moon is in the sixth, and both of them are afflicted by Mars in the first house, whose radical place and [that of] the Moon was on the eighth cusp of that same revolution. therefore, from these [positions] a violent illness and one with danger or fear of death is

---

[19] I suppose that he is referring to the remarks Cardan made about the nativity of Alexander I de' Medici, Duke of Florence, who was born 7 Feb 1512 according to Luca Gaurico, *Tractatus astrologicus* (Venice, 1552), the 190th chart (see NN 527) and was murdered on 5/6 Jan 1537. He was a bastard son of Pope Clement VII (1478-1534).

13

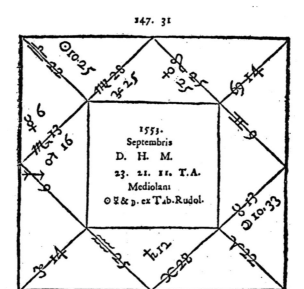

Cardan's 53rd Revolution[20]
24 September 1553
9:11 AM LAT

plainly signified, as [indeed] it happened. But perhaps Cardan did not inspect the figure of the revolution, for sometimes he judges the year from the revolution, and sometimes without it, as we said above. Therefore, he only attributes that illness to the monthly progressions of the ASC and the Moon to their oppositions on that very day and to the transits of the planets through the places of the nativity at the initial moment of the illness, the figure of which is shown below.

In which in fact the ASC is in opposition to the radical Venus and Mercury,[21] which along with the Sun were in the sixth,

---

[20] The RAMC is 147°31' not 247°31' as it may appear to be.

[21] Morin is referring to the positions of Mercury, Venus, and the Sun that were in Libra in the 6th house of Cardan's horoscope. That chart is not given here, but it is shown on p. 195 of my translation of Book 23.

Figura Morbi.

214. 1

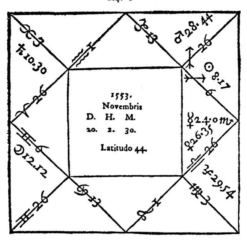

1553.
Novembris
D. H. M.
20. 2. 30.

Latitudo 44

Figure of an Illness
20 November 1553
2:30 PM LAT

significators of illnesses; and this was certainly bad, but [even] worse with the direction of Sun mentioned above, since Saturn was in the twelfth transiting the [radical] Moon,[22] and he was square his own radical place and the radical place of Mars, and in the twelfth house of the figure, which is per se [the house] of illnesses. These transits, therefore, were very bad, and along with them the figure was also very bad, which here I only want to note in passing, to be explained more fully at another time, and all these things agreeing greatly on illness, which Cardan himself experienced with danger or at least with the fear of death, on account of the Sun and Mars, rulers of the ASC, the latter of which is in the eighth afflicted by the square of Saturn from the twelfth, and the former afflicted by the square of Jupiter, ruler of the eighth, from the sixth house.

---

[22] In Cardan's horoscope, the Moon was located in 11 ♓ 42 in the 11th house.

15

But because he is looking at those progressions, I am especially looking for the reason why he wanted the day of the effect to be indicated by the monthly progressions rather than by the annual ones, since the annual ones are prior and more powerful for the particulars and also for defining the times, as Cardan himself will have it in his *Book of Revolutions*, Chapter 8, just as the monthly ones prevail over the daily ones? Besides, since in that same Book, Chapter 13, he investigates the days of the events from the directions of the revolutions that he thought up and were rejected by me in Book 22, Chapter 15. If those directions were seen to be true in themselves, what need was there for the progressions? Or if the latter were true, what need was there for those directions? The superfluousness of one or the other of the methods is evident, and consequently confusion in judgments must arise. Besides, in Cardan's example the ASC in its annual progression was then in 10 degrees 46 minutes of Virgo, still distant from the opposition of the radical Moon by more than 10 days; but the Moon was in 16 degrees and 18 minutes of Cancer, where nothing was found, and consequently not with annual progressions coinciding with the time; Cardan assumed the monthly ones to be much swifter, which by chance coincided. And this egregious coincidence (the sort of thing that often happens) can deceive those who do not know that these progressions do not rest upon any real foundation and are of three sorts, some swifter than the others; moreover, they still ignore the other real causes, namely, the directions of the solar and lunar revolutions that we have explained, which designate the very particular times of the effects, if not exactly to the day and hour, at least closely, as will now be plain in this illness of Cardan's, since in fact in the figure of the annual revolution Mercury and the Moon, are from what was said above, the significators of illnesses and death and do therefore act with regard to illnesses, like the promissors in the annual direction meeting them. Moreover, Mercury according to the *Rudolphine Tables* was in the 6th degree of Scorpio with 3 degrees and 8 minutes of South latitude, and the altitude of the pole above its circle of position was 44°30′; therefore, its oblique ascension was 228°45',[23] which subtracted from the oblique ascension of the opposition to Saturn in the radix, which is according to the *Rudolphine Tables* 20°20' of Gemini with latitude 1°28' South (which ascension in the above said altitude is 282°45')[24] leaves 54 degrees for the arc of direction, which from the Table of annual directions equals 55 days; moreover, from the beginning of the revolution to the illness was 57 days.[25]

Similarly, the Moon from the *Rudolphine Tables* is found in 10°33' of Taurus with latitude 4°36' South, and the pole is 44 degrees above its circle of position; therefore, the oblique ascension of the opposition to the Moon is 230 degrees, which subtracted from the opposition to the radical Saturn, [whose] oblique ascension is 282°22' leaves 52°12' for the arc of direction, [which] equals 53 days.[26]

Therefore, the direction of the Moon to the place of the radical Saturn preceded the illness by around 3 days; and the direction of Mercury to that same opposition of Saturn preceded the illness by only 2 days; moreover, the directions of Mercury and the Moon to the place and the opposition of Saturn in the ecliptic were still closer to the effect. Wherefore, all of these together produced an illness in the Native by their own influxes, or they excited the la-

---

[23] Actually, according to the *Rudolphine Tables*, Mercury was at about 5°27' Scorpio 3S12, and its OA for an altitude of 44°30' was 228°51'.

[24] Reading the Gemini symbol rather than the square symbol in the Latin text The position of Saturn according to the *Rudolphine Tables* was actually about 18°36' Gemini 1S35, and the OA of its opposition was 280°26'.

[25] I calculate for altitude 44°30' Mercury OA 228°51' and for the opposition to Saturn OA 280°26'; hence, their difference is 51°35' (as compared with the 54°00' obtained by Morin).

[26] Here, for the stated coordinates of the Moon, the recalculated OA of the Moon is 230°03' for an altitude of 44°00'; and its difference firom the recalculated OA of the opposition to Saturn (280°26') is 50°23' (as compared to Morin's 50°12'). When converted into days, the previous calculation and this differ from Morin's figures by 3 and 2 days respectively, but the recalculated figures are still not far from the actual 57 days to the accident.

tent seeds of it; and they disposed Cardan himself very close to the threatening effect; but finally, from the above said transits coming on top [of these], the illness was reduced from potentiality to actuality; it broke out violently and suddenly as it were because of the strength and malignity of the transits, especially from the concordant situation of the Planets in the figure for the breaking out of the illness; for the transits are only actual causes, and therefore activating ones, or ones inducing the forms of the effects; and so it is in all other things, for nature has a universal method of operating to which all things are subject.

I omit [the fact] that in the figure of the periodic revolution of the Moon, which preceded the illness by 7 days,[27] erected from the *Ephemerides* of Pitatus[28] which Cardan himself used in the figure above, and that to the radical place of the Moon 11°42' of Pisces, as he himself puts it in his nativity; the Moon and Saturn are conjoined in the ASC and square Mars ruler of the eighth. And the ASC with the Moon and Saturn are directed in the monthly mode on the very day of the illness to the dexter square of the place of the radical Sun, which, in the 6th house of the radix, was the significator of illnesses, which direction was very sickly.

Besides, the worthlessness of the progressions will plainly be more evident for whoever will want to experiment with them, when he has used the genuine and proper significators of the effects, whose progressions are made to concordant promissors, for he will see that they agree with those effects only rarely and coincidentally, and not always all of them, but now the annual ones, now the monthly ones, and now the daily ones, which cannot be said of the revolutions and their directions set forth by us in Book 23, and whose verity anyone will experience in any other examples. And

---

[27] This lunar revolution occurred a few minutes after 1:00 LMT on 13 November 1553. The Moon and Saturn were rising in Pisces square Mars in Sagittarius in the MC, and Mars was ruler of the 8th house.

[28] Petrus Pitatns, *Almanach novum...* (Tübingen: Ulrich Morhard, 1544), an ephemeris for the years 1551-1556. See Thorndike, HMES 5, pp. 264-265.

18

consequently, since only by chance is there a concourse of the progressions at the times of the effects, and since they are not based upon any real foundation, we are of the opinion that they by rights ought to be eliminated from Astrology.

And it is not because someone may pretend that the annual direction, whose daily motion is 59′, almost equal to the monthly profection, whose daily motion is 64′04″, and similarly the monthly direction, whose daily motion is 13°10′35″, are almost equivalent to the daily progression, whose daily motion is 13°52′52″; and consequently, there is no great difference between our directions and the progressions of the Old [Astrologers]. For first, the significator in the annual direction runs completely through the Zodiac in a solar year; but in the monthly progressions it runs completely through 13 signs without any reason other than that it was pleasing to their author. The annual and monthly progressions for individual years begins from the same point of the Zodiac; similarly, the significator in the monthly direction in its monthly period runs through the whole Zodiac completely; but in the daily progression it runs through 13 signs in a profectional month – this only from the cause, that in the beginnings of the individual profectional months the point of the *Caelum* of each significator is the same for the monthly and diurnal profections because it was pleasing to the inventor of these to play with so many numbers. Second, the directions are by a natural mode related to the circles of position, but the progressions only to a fictitious and equal [mode] in the ecliptic; and because these progressions are only a twelfth part swifter than our directions, and because the latter proceed unequally, but the former equally, it is no wonder that sometimes they imitate the true causes, especially in the beginnings of years and months. Add [to this] that the same places of the Sun and the Moon in the ecliptic are directed in revolutions of the Sun and Moon as those which are advanced monthly and daily by the progressions, namely the radical places of the Sun and the Moon. Third [and] finally, because for the annual and monthly directions the significators for directing are chosen only in figures of the revolutions of the Sun and the Moon. But for progressions the significators are only taken from the figure of the nativity; therefore, the directions that have been adopted by us differ greatly from the progressions of the Old [Astrologers], concerning which what has been said so far is sufficient.

SECTION II.
The Transits and the Syzygies of the Planets.

Chapter 1.
How Should the Doctrine of Transits be Made.

Even though this doctrine is the last in order in the Theory of Astrology; that is, it is about the celestial causes both ultimate and particular of all the effects happening to a man; it is not, however, the last in nobility, since indeed it embraces all the other preceding things and is the crown of them, sparkling with the most beautiful ideas, as will be shown in what follows. Because there are those not understanding, and there are many who have conceded [only] a minimum of virtue for the production of effects to transits among the [other] celestial causes, supposing those [causes] to be rather from directions or from progressions, which we have rejected in the first chapter, and not taking note that for any particular effect, supposing such a one is from celestial causes, the celestial cause ought to be a particular active one, which schemes of the nativity and its directions are not, nor are revolutions and their directions, which, with respect to future accidents at least, are potential causes subordinated to themselves, as we have said in Books 22 and 23. Consequently, others are superior to them and more universal, tending ordinarily to some particular which is entirely active, by which that which is potential in them is reduced to an action. Moreover, such a cause is the transit of the Planets through concordant places of the figures, both of the radix and of a revolution, as will be more fully stated below.

Furthermore, Ptolemy himself commends this doctrine at the end of the last chapter of the *Quadripartite*, declaring that the force of a decree, that is the active force of the stars, the producer of the effects, begins to shine forth then when concordant transits of the Planets are made or aspects of the Sun or of the Moon through the annual or monthly signs; that is those that are occupied by significators in the annual or monthly progression. But in his *Com-*

mentary Cardan also wants it to be understood that a diurnal progression was propounded by that same Ptolemy. But because we have rejected those progressions as worthless, and seeing that we were only mentioning those annual and monthly directions that we have introduced, as we have said in Section I, Chapter 3; consequently, they must be preferred to those others by the best judgment. For in fact it is absurd to think that any significator in the natal figure is progressed by a fourfold motion in that chart, namely by the motion of a radical direction, then by an annual, monthly and daily progression. But enough about this already! Here we only intend to show that Ptolemy himself discovered a significant force in transits when they were made through concordant or discordant places in the nativity, and thus to conclude that the doctrine of transits should be manifold, and that there is a significant force in the transits by body or by aspect of the seven Planets, but especially of the Sun and the Moon.

Chapter 2.
What Path Previous Astrologers Followed in Taking Notice of the Virtue of the Stars.

It seems appropriate here to imitate the Prince of Alchemy, the very wise Isaac Hollandus,[29] in Book 20 of his *Operum Mineralium*, where in Chapter 98 he learnedly expounds the ways by which the Old Chemists arrived at a perfect understanding of the art of transmutation by erecting [theories] and trying [them] out.

It must be known therefore that it was known by the ancient Astrologers, [to whom it was] made clear by the light of Philosophy, that not only is the *Caelum* the active effector of those things which are already done on things sublunar, but it is also potentially the effector of those things that are going to be, since they cannot be done without a concurring *Caelum*. Moreover, the kinds of fu-

---

[29] John Isaac Hollandus, a writer on alchemy in the first half of the 17th century.

ture accidents, such as heat, cold, flood, sterility, pestilence, war, and similar things, are not made by some particular concourse and position of the stars, with experience as a witness, but only by [something] certain and determined, which, since in essence it depends upon the motion of those stars at a definitely determined time, it then follows that from a particular constitution of the *Caelum* it can be conjectured at what time any particular accident may occur, if we can estimate at what time there will be a concourse of the stars suitable to producing that [accident].

When, therefore, the Old [Astrologers] from the different sites of the Planets in the zodiac, diverse among themselves and combined with the fixed [stars], and with diverse sites of them and of the whole *Caelum* with respect to the horizon, they would judge all these inferior things to be changed, and especially the more significant changes to happen around the times of the great conjunctions, of the annual revolutions, of eclipses, and lunations. It seemed proper to them to erect celestial figures at the moments of those configurations, and from the contemplation of these to inquire into the types, causes, and times of impending or near future changes. And to be sure they were experienced in observing that the kinds and causes of events depended on the nature and celestial and terrestrial state of the Planets of the predominating configuration; and the times were determined by the distances of those rulers from the principal places of the configuration, or from themselves in turn. And consequently, the effects of that same configuration did not appear at the very moment of that configuration, except perhaps very rarely, namely when there is no such distance, since they depend on being done by a time on account of that distance; but only their seeds are enclosed in the influences of the stars; then, they are shot into the womb of Sublunar nature, quickly or slowly to be brought into the light, according as the aforesaid distance was greater or less. And at that time to be produced, in which the rulers of the constitution, discovered by lengthy observations, were transiting through its principal places by their own motion, or they were applying to themselves, even though the Planets that held those places at the moment of that constitution were far away from them at the very time of the transits. For these reasons, they admired the force of the transits very much.

Moreover, when they would consider those things in the universal constitutions of the *Caelum* and in the changes of sublunar things, they also began to think about particulars. And since they knew that man excelled all other things, for whose special grace the *Caelum* itself and all the Earth was created, they judged the prevision of illnesses and other accidents to be very important for the preservation of that man—to know under what position of the *Caelum* and the stars he would be born. For with the *Caelum* posited [as] the cause of the generation and the corruption of sublunar things, it is reasonably especially fitting that a man is altered or even corrupted by a [celestial] constitution contrary to that one by which he was generated, since whatever is preserved by a similar one is likewise destroyed by a contrary one.

Therefore, having erected a celestial figure at the moment and place of a nativity, first they learned from it the constitution of the Native's body, then whether this will be healthy, or the dangers of illnesses; but afterwards they inquired as to what illnesses and at what time. And in fact they found the kinds and causes of illnesses, then of other effects, from the natures of the Planets and signs and their situation in the figure, or they exerted themselves even more profoundly by defining the times of the accidents of life. For the simple transits of the Planets through the principal places of the natal figure were not always producing the signified accidents, as in universal constitutions, but only on occasion, and [even] that rarely; for if transits alone were sufficient, since the Moon twelve times in a year is together with Mercury, Venus, and the Sun; and Jupiter, Saturn, and Mars many times during [a person's] life transit all the places of the natal figure, [then] as many times as the transits return, so many times also would the accidents signified by them return, and yet this was not discovered to be done. However, they have held it as a thing very certain that the signified accidents cannot be produced except by an actually concurring concordant influx of its own efficient cause; wherefore, they wisely supposed that concordant transits of the Planets are indeed absolutely necessary [to serve] as actual influxes for the production of signified events; these, however, can scarcely produce [those events] unless there is a concurrent cause at a certain time, which however, is determined by the distance of the significator of the event from one of its promissors; for they do not doubt that the kind of event depends on the natures of those [planets] and on both their celestial and terrestrial state [and] likewise its time determined by the distance between them.

But nevertheless, they learned by daily observations that that distance is measured in the equator by the mean daily motion of the Sun with respect to that circle, which is 59′08″,[30] so that however many mean daily motions of the Sun, the promissor by the motion of the *Primum Mobile,* or in degrees of the equator, is distant from the circle of position of the significator, to which by that same motion it was proceeding in the hour of the nativity—in that same number of years the effect signified by the concourse of the significator and the promissor would follow after the nativity. Consequently, the equation of the years of the Native with the daily [motions] of the Sun intercepted in that distance,[31] by that cause would be slower, than it would necessarily be with concordant transits concurring.

And then, moreover, having added speculations about the Native's annual revolutions, in likeness of the years of the world,[32] they eventually established for themselves a universal science of the virtue of the stars on these inferior things. For the very oldest

---

[30] The so-called Naibod Measure of Time.

[31] The "daily [motions] intercepted m that distance" is an elegant way of saying "the arc of direction."

[32] The "years of the world" are what we would call ''Aries ingresses'' today.

Astrologers do not seem to have erected annual revolutions, since Ptolemy makes no mention of them;[33] therefore, such was the progress of the Old [Astrologers] in the recognition of the virtue of the stars with regard to general and particular effects.

Chapter 3.
Whether the Transits of All the Planets Through the Individual Places of the Nativity should be Observed.

The *places* of nativities are of two kinds, for some are the places of significators, namely the places of the 7 Planets, the 12 [house] cusps, and the Part of Fortune, but others are the places of promissors, namely the places of the 7 Planets, their aspects, and antiscions. For each planet in a nativity is simultaneously a significator and a promissor, looked at diversely, namely a significator of those things to which it was determined by its bodily position and its rulership, but a promissor of those things to which it was potentially determined by its directions to preceding significators.

Since, therefore, the natal constitution and its directions are, with respect to the Native, something potential for the future things [that will happen] to that same Native, which are indicated by the significators as well as by the promissors—for such future things do not pass from potentiality into actuality, or from being in the future to an actual existence without the concurrence of actual causes, which Astrologers have observed in very frequent experiments to be the transits of the Planets acting in accordance with their own radical signification along with that of the houses in combination— in general, it follows that since all the Planets make their transits through the individual places of the nativity, and are able to combine with the individual [Planets], the transits of all of

---

[33] This is true. It was apparently one of the 8th century Arabian astrologers who invented the solar revolution (solar return).

them through the individual places of the nativity must also be looked at, not only transits by body but also by aspect.

Moreover, it must be noted that just as the effects of directions are from the *Primum Mobile*, therefore their times should be measured by the ascensions of the promissor in the site of the significator; thus, the effects of transits are from the second or individual motion of the transiting Planets; therefore, the times of the effects [resulting] from transits should be measured by the individual motion of the transiting Planets.

Besides, a transiting planet must be considered not with just any kind of consideration, but there are three considerations that must be particularly noticed. First, what is its own particular nature, for it is not sufficient to know that a transiting planet is by nature a benefic or a malefic; but one ought to know whether it is Jupiter or Venus, or in fact Saturn or Mars, because indeed Jupiter has one nature and Venus has another, just as Saturn has one and Mars has another, each one of which moreover acts in accordance with its own nature. Second, what is its radical determination, for it will act in a transit according to that. For this reason, the transit of Mars through the vital places of the nativity, [when it is] determined to death or to illnesses in the radix, is dangerous to life or to health. Third, what is the celestial state of the transiting planet at the time of the transit—that is, is it concordant or non-concordant with its radical signification, and with the combination of that which was signified by the place through which it is transiting. Then, whether it is strong or weak, for [a planet that is] concordant and strong may act strongly for good or evil, [but one that is] non-concordant for nothing, especially when it is weak.

And not just those three [things] must be considered in the case of a transiting Planet, but also the Planet or the cusp of the house through the place of which it is making its transit at the very time of the transit. For, since the signs were determined from the beginning of the world to the natures of the Planets, they act depending on the state of their own rulers, as we have said in Book

20, Section 3, Chapters 2 and 4, so the places of the *Caelum* in the radix that were particularly determined by the Planets act on the Native during the [entire] course of his life depending on the state of the Planets determining; consequently, the transit of Jupiter through the ASC of the radix at which time Venus, ruler of the ASC, is in exile and retrograde, and impedited by the rays of the malefics, Saturn or Mars, will bring forth very little or even nothing.

But from that is deduced this—which is very much worth noting—namely, that if the figure was erected by the Equal [House] system, or another false one,[34] errors will unavoidably occur in connection with predictions [based] on transits; namely, because the degrees of the Planets and the cusps will be thought to be in one house of the figure, when in fact they are in another, and consequently determined otherwise in the radix than he may may think, who erected the figure in a false system.

Chapter 4.
Whether in an Individual House of the Nativity any Force Exceeds [that of the] Natal Chart for Future Accidents of Life.

Although we have already spoken about this matter in Book 20, Section 3, Chapter 5, and then in Book 21, Section 1, Chapter 4, still because there is nothing in Astrology that man's talent means to hold more equal in admiration than that a planet transiting a place that was one of the cusps of the natal figure, especially one of the cardinal cusps, or a place that any Planet held at

---

[34] The Equal House system had been used by Cardan; and it had also been adopted by Morin's contemporary, Nicolas de Bourdin, the Marquess of Villennes (d. 1670). The other "false" systems according to Morin's opinion were the Alchabitius system and the Campanus system He had denounced all of these in earlier books of the AG and also in his separate work, *Remarques Astrologiques* (Paris: Pierre Menard, 1657), which, like the AG, was published after Morin's death in 1656.

the hour of the nativity, acts according to the signification of that same house or to the particular signification of the Planet in the radix; even though at the very moment of that transit, the other Planet that occupied that place is absent, and moreover, the consideration of this effect is the principal foundation of the doctrine of transits, consequently then, lest anything concerning it be lacking, we may put here that which will seem to be sufficient for a clearer understanding of the virtue of those transits; for we promised [to do] this in Books 20 and 21.

Therefore, such an effect does not arise from those things because there remains in that very *Caelum* the virtue of a previously located Planet impressed according to its form, either universal and common to all the world from its own form, or particular, from the particular situation of the Planet in the figure with respect to the man who is being born. Not universal, for through the whole zodiac which that Planet traverses, it remains in the same mode; consequently, the observation of those places for transits would be useless, for it would take on equally the same effect in one and another point of the zodiac, of course because the individual points of the zodiac would be equal in that sort of virtue; but this disagrees with experience. But not so the particular mentioned above; for since all the inhabitants of the earth have the same planet at the same moment of time in the same point of the *Caelum*, and yet the Planet does not effect the same thing in [all] the individual men then being born; but in this one it acts on his life, in that one on his finances, etc.; [and] it would follow all the virtues, or all the particular modes, of that same Planet impressed according to its form upon that same point of the *Caelum* that it can exercise with respect to a [particular] man. Therefore, that virtue that is impressed is not particular but universal, because in fact all the particulars are equivalent to the universal. Wherefore, if a transit operates according to this virtue impressed according to its form, there will be no reason why from a transit there would follow in this [particular] man an effect on his life rather than on his finances, or his honors, etc., but [the answer] would have to be sought from somewhere else—see Book 20, Section 3, chapter 5, where it is shown in detail that the *Caelum* receives nothing from the Planets according to their form. But the matter is as follows.

The *Primum Mobile* is the first and the most universal cause of all natural effects. But these are not from the *Caelum* alone, because of itself it is determined to no type of effect; but they are also from the Planets, by which the *Caelum* itself was determined universally to the signs at the beginning of the world, and it is determined particularly on each day, both by its own motion around the earth and by the Planets' own motions, as we have said in Book 21, Chapter 4. And [these effects] are not also from the Planets alone; for Mars has one effect in Aries, or with Aries, and another in Taurus; they are, therefore, effects from the mutual concourse of the *Caelum* and the Planets. And yet the primacy of efficiency is due to the *Caelum*, as the prime cause in physics of all things, shown by us in Book 14, Section 1, Chapter 1; for as GOD effectively concurred with every created agent, as the first cause of causes, without which nothing can be done, so the *Primum Mobile* (the noblest image of God) concurs with every natural agent, as the prime physical cause, without which, even with the Sun itself remaining along with the other Planets, universal nature would languish, on account of the formal virtue of the *Caelum* itself, [which is] like the mind or the spirit, penetrating, vivifying, and preserving the whole corporeal world.

Furthermore, even if they are given in these inferiors subjects passive in form and equal to the rest, the *Primum Caelum* does not, however, always effect the same thing in individuals; the same thing, therefore, does not remain in individuals; for *the same remaining the same, does the the same thing in the same*; however, the same remains in individuals in nature, or in formal virtue, for the nature and virtue of the *Primum Caelum* are immutable, because it is the prime cause, subordinate to no other effecting agent, but it does not remain the same in the location of its degrees, for this is continually varied by the continuous motion of the *Caelum* itself, and it is made diverse for individuals by reason of the degrees. Therefore, the diversity of the situation of the *Caelum* itself with respect to individual men at the moment of birth will be a cause on the part of the *Primum Mobile* of the diversity of effects in those same men—namely, one of whom has Aries in the ASC, another Taurus, etc.

The same thing must be said about any Planet, which in the same moment of time is the same for individual sublunar subjects in nature and in universal virtue, but diverse for them in its situation; whence, its universal nature determined variously by its situation with respect to individuals that are being born, does also in the same instant of time produce different effects in individuals. And in addition, it determines the part of the *Primum Caelum* under which it is seen from the earth to its own nature and virtue, both [what is] essential from its own nature and accidental from its situation with respect to the Native, with such great efficacy that that part of the *Caelum* itself under which the Sun is seen, is to that very Native during his whole life like another Sun, and one similarly determined by reason of the house of the figure, as was the Sun itself in the nativity; whence, it can be said not undeservedly that in that impression of the celestial constitution, which the Native receives at birth, the Planet is like a certain mean proportion between the *Caelum* and the Native, connecting both of them.

Therefore, since the Primum *Mobile* and those stars that are moving under it, in accordance with the diversity of their own determination with respect to the individual Natives, produce diverse effects in the individuals; to be sure it follows that of whatever sort each of them is in body, talents, habits, and luck, such a sort emerged from the virtue and determination of the celestial bodies with respect to the moment of his own birth; and having received the impression of this celestial constitution, the Native incurs sympathy and antipathy with the *Caelum*, and consequently with universal nature, so that just as the production of the Native himself depends upon that constitution, so does his preservation, since it consists of such a situation of the celestial bodies with respect to the Native; and it is well affected in turn by the characteristic and common motion of the Planets. And from this it follows that the alteration and corruption of the Native himself will be from a contrary constitution or situation of the celestial bodies.

Moreover, a contrary situation can occur in three ways. First, that the situation of the *Caelum* is the same, but that of the planets is contrary—that is, the same degree or sign of the zodiac ascends above the horizon of the Native that ascended in his nativity, but all the planets are in opposition to their own radical places. Second, that the planets are disposed in the *Caelum* just as they were in the nativity, but the *Caelum* is in an entirely opposite mode. Third, that the situation of both the *Caelum* as well as that of the Planets is plainly contrary to their radical situations—and this is the worst of all. But a subcontrary can happen in just as many modes, and a related one in just as many; for the situation of the *Caelum* with respect to the horizon alone is noted, but also the situation of the Planets with respect to that *Caelum*, under which they revolve with their own motions.

Since, therefore, a man may be born in the middle of ten sites[35] differing in virtue among themselves, which they have called houses, through which the celestial bodies pour out all the kinds of accidents that are appropriate for man, as we have said in Book 18, Section 1, Chapters 2 & 3, it must be seen in the nativity of each man how the *Primum Caelum* may be divided among those sites, and which are the places both of the divisions of it, and also of the Planets in it. For of whatever sort were the parts of the *Caelum*, or the *Dodecatemorion*,[36] and the Planet by body, rulership, or aspect, occupying each house, the Native receives that sort of active or passive power for the accidents signified by that house and that much sympathy with that sort of celestial constitution, so

---

[35] The Latin has *in medio decem situum* 'in the middle of ten sites', but since he seems to be referring to the twelve houses, perhaps we should emend the text to read *in medio duodecim situum* 'in the middle of twelve sites'.

[36] By *dodecatemorion* he means simply a twelfth part of the *Caelum*, i.e. one of the twelve houses.

that however often any change happens in it, that many times also does a change happen for the Native in the thing or kind of accident signified by that house; if at least the change of constitution was concordant with the directions and revolutions, which was mentioned above. Moreover, a change happens in the houses of that constitution in two ways. First, from the motion of the *Primum Mobile*, which carries those houses around daily through the individual sites. Second, from the motion of the Planets, by which the Moon once in each month; Mercury, Venus, and the Sun once in each year; Mars once in two years; Jupiter once in twelve; and Saturn once in 30 years transits those individual places. Moreover, a change alone of a site with respect to the earth or from the *Primum Mobile* is of no efficacy for sublunar changes because it does not alter the universal nature's force of acting. For, always posited in the same site among themselves, the universal nature of the stars, notwithstanding the diurnal motion of the *Caelum* that would change the force of acting; and consequently remaining the same, it would always effect the same thing. But by the variation of the situation of the Planets with respect to the *Caelum* by their own individual motions, there happens [to be] in universal nature a diversity of the virtue of acting; for from that variation of situation the syzygies of the Planets occur among themselves and with the fixed [stars]—some of them translations from one sign into another, through which the celestial bodies act in various ways on all these sublunar things [but] only universally; with the Planets continuously determining with respect to the individuals who are being born, the points of the *Primum Mobile* under which they are seen from the earth.

But when a Planet transits by its own motion through a point of the *Caelum*, already determined by the radix with respect to the Native to the nature of another Planet, or its aspect, or to a cusp; and so the transiting Planet comes into the radical place of another [Planet], the radical constitution of that Native is disturbed, both the celestial one and the impressed one, on account of the sympathy brought about, even as the universal nature would be disturbed if, with any one of the 7 Planets removed, another one of a different nature made up anew were substituted in place of it, especially if there is a great contrariety either in their natures or in the significations of the Planet transiting the radical and of the one through whose radical place it is transiting. For every Planet, led around in the zodiac by its own motion, retains with respect to the Native so long as he lives its radical or accidental virtue from its radical determination, and with that it continually acts upon the Native—imperceptibly to be sure when it transits through the empty places of the nativity, that is, those which are not cusps or the places of the Planets, or the places of aspects in the radical constitution; but perceptibly when it transits through those places or cusps, especially if the transit is noteworthy and there is a concordant direction and revolution, as will be stated more fully below. For then from such a transit an effect signified by a direction of the nativity and [also] by a revolution is reduced from a potentiality to an actuality—there having been set in motion the active or the passive causes of that effect intrinsic to the Native, but extrinsic in the universal nature, that is in the *Caelum* or in sublunar things, so that something happens to the Native of the kind of signification pertaining to the place through which the transit is [made]. But when some Planet transits through its own radical location, in that way the effect that is radically signified by it bursts forth.

Besides, when a Planet transits through some point of the *Caelum* already determined by the nativity, it must be seen whether both determinations, namely the determinations of the transiting Planet and of the radical point are similar or agreeing in the same effect with a concordant state of the transiting Planet; for given this, the effect will be produced immediately, according to the signification of the place or of the point of the *Caelum* determined by the radix, through which it is transiting. But if the determinations were contrary, because the transiting Planet, either by its own nature, or by its radical signification, were contrary to the radical determination of the place through which it is transiting, then damages, impediments, [and] misfortunes are signified. And with a malefic Planet transiting through a good place, evil rushes into the good; but with a benefic transiting through an evil [place], good falls upon the evil.

Moreover, because transiting Planets [alone] are not sufficient for an effect, they are in their own site or that of another with respect to the earth by the *Primum Mobile*, but in general it is necessary that it be in its own place or in that of another with respect to the *Primum Caelum*; hence it is plainly evident that not only is the *Caelum* itself the prime and most efficacious of all the physical causes, with everything else concurring, but in addition in that place through which there is a transit the force surviving from the nativity is the producer at a concordant time of future effects for the Native. Otherwise, there would be no reason why Mars, ruler of the eighth, transiting by body or by a malefic aspect through the ASC or the place of the ruler of the ASC, might rather cause an illness or a danger to life than when it is transiting through some other degree of the zodiac. For since effects are apprehended from concordant transits, it ought to be that the force from these belongs to those. But two celestial causes concur for a transit, namely that of the transiting Planet and [that of] the place or part of the *Primum Caelum* through which it is transiting. Moreover, the virtue productive of the effect should not be viewed differently from any other cause; otherwise, the Planet could either always and everywhere produce the same effect or always produce it from the same place; or at least it would be done by the transit of some other Planet; both of which experience proves to be false. Moreover, it is from the concourse of both causes, also with experience as a witness; therefore, it is necessary that the virtue belongs incompletely to both causes viewed separately, but completely to both concurring together; whence, it is also plain that each cause concurs in the production of the effect with its own radical determination, which consequently also still survives in the transiting Planet, which is most worthy of note.

Besides, it was said above that the Native draws together the sympathy and antipathy with the *Caelum* from the impression of the celestial constitution received at the moment of his nativity, and then with nature combined, which I want to be extended all the way, so that it can also be understood with the individual natal constitutions of the Natives, and through them with the Natives themselves, or rather with all the sublunar things subordinate to the rulership of the celestial bodies. For it is frequently observed that in any particular accident signified especially by external causes, very many causes, among them [those of] various kinds, come together at the same time—generally very different in motions and modes—of which not a single one is superfluous for the effect. But all of them are necessary, so that, with any one of them lacking, it would seem that the effect could not be produced, as is plain in the death of Julius Caesar, Henry IV King of France, Gustavus Adolphus King of Sweden, and in innumerable other cases, which do not occur by chance (as the ignorant suppose) but by fatal providence, and they seize men by surprise. But by a single direction, also with a revolution and a concordant transit in the nativity of an individual man, so many causes agreeing mutually to be moved toward the effect and to come together at the same time, or through the Native's own constitution, the wonderful sympathy or antipathy with universal nature, as explained above, and in many nativities of other men, seem to be naturally impossible, since there does not appear to be any other natural reason.

Chapter 5.
Whether all the Transits Through the Places of the Nativity are Effective, or Whether they Alone and in some Way Motivate our own Nature to the Effects.

That all the transits through the places of the nativity are not efficacious is proved most evidently by the primary planets, the Sun and the Moon, [and they are] primary among the other [planets], for the Sun transits all the houses of the nativity every year and the Moon every month; and yet effects do not happen to the native in every year, much less in every month, at least not conspicuous ones with individual significations in his own nativity. Therefore, there is required a concourse of that later cause, which was mentioned in Chapter 2, certainly of a direction and a revolution concordant with a transit; for the effects result from a mutual concord of causes, just as a dissension or contrariety of causes impedes them, so that nothing that is notable and complete is produced. Therefore, even though the Planets are transiting the places of the nativity by their own motion, they always do with those same places whatever they can both by reason of their own nature and by reason of their own radical determination; consequently, Venus transiting through the ASC by her own nature alone excites [the Native] to pleasures and jokes, but more effectively if she was the ruler of habits or of the fifth [house]; and yet without any direction and concordant revolution, or at least by one of these concordant with the nativity, it will not cause any notable change in the Native; but this is only done by transits when concordant directions and revolutions concur with them.

Moreover, Kepler wanted to define how these transits disturb our nature, asserting that the Planets and the other celestial bodies do not actually disturb human nature but only apparently.[37] And afterwards, he acknowledged that in the natural and animal faculties of a child being born there is received the constitution of the *Caelum* which at the time of its rising was made on his faculties through the impression by that same *Caelum*; and from this he will have it that at the [time of] transits of the Planets through the principal places of the nativity the faculty excites itself, as if the images received in the mind at the moment of birth were true stars coexisting and agreeing or disagreeing with the celestial ones; of course, he will have a faculty necessarily intent upon observations of the motions of the celestial bodies, so that throughout the whole life of the man it regulates its own works, which are the accidents that are going to be for that man. But we have refuted Kepler's opinion in Book 21, Section 1, Chapters 4-7, and then in Book 22, Section 3,

---

[37] The Latin text has *non efficienter, sed duntaxat objectivè*, lit. 'not efficiently, but only objectively', but here I think Kepler meant 'not actually...but only apparently', as I have rendered it.

Chapter 2, to which places we refer the Reader.

On the other hand, we say that all living things make use of a twofold physical food, that is they feed on what is material, and they are ruled by what is spiritual; but the spiritual is none other than Air, since it is impregnated with celestial influences, which men take in copiously by breathing along with the rest of the animals. But the celestial influences are noticeably varied with respect to each man, according as the Planets in individual nativities transit through the principal places of the natal chart, with a concurrent and especially a concordant direction and revolution. Whence, it is true that the air which, impregnated by those influences, is drawn in, may move the natural desire of man toward those things, or to doing those things, or enduring them. For thus at birth you will come to the first breathing in of the influx of the celestial configuration [that] is imprinted on the Native, and by which he is generally endowed, both for the accidents present at that instant and for future ones during the course of his life.

You will object: It will follow that all those who breathe in the same air at the time of such a transit are similarly moved to acting or experiencing. But since this is repugnant to experience, not only in the same region or city, but also in the same dwelling, this doctrine is therefore absurd.

I reply. What is objected to does not follow. For instance, from the transit of Mars through the same degree of the zodiac, it does not follow that all men are similarly affected, but only those who by reason of their own natal chart have sympathy or antipathy with Mars and with that degree. So that, if for any Native that degree is his ASC, and Mars is the ruler of his eighth or twelfth, such a Native will be afflicted by illness or by a danger to his life, but not another person, who, with such a degree and Mars, did not incur the sympathy or antipathy of life, of illnesses, or of death, although for all of them Mars is in that same degree. For the air itself is not harmful to all those breathing it, just as Mars transiting through that degree is not harmful to all of them, although its universal influx affects all of them. And from this it is plain that those breathing the same air can be affected through sympathy with the celestial bodies perpetually acting upon that same air, sometimes in the same way, and at other times in different ways, or even in a harmful way.

Chapter 6.
Whether the Transiting Planets Determine the Place of their own Transits, or Whether They are Determined by Them, and in what Way.

The planets moved by their own proper motion under the *Primum Mobile* actively determine its parts to their own nature with respect to sublunar things; and in turn, they are determined by the *Caelum*, or by its parts, and they act as associates just as was said in Book 21, Section 1, Chapter 5. Again, therefore, in [the case of] transits, the transiting Planet and the place through which it transits determine each other mutually with respect to the native; not indeed in a simple manner, but with regard to their own prior determinations in the nativity; e.g., Mars ruler of the 8th, transiting through the places of the ASC and its ruler, determines these not only to the Martian nature (which is a simple determination), but it also determines them to death, or to [some] danger to life, namely because Mars by its own determination in the radix produced the force of death for the native. Moreover, it cannot exert that force more effectively on the Native than by transiting by body, or by a hostile aspect, through the places of the radical figure that are determined to life, such as the ASC and its ruler are; for the radical places, when they are determined by a transit to significations contrary to their radical ones, then a change in the radical signification must be feared for the Native; and because when Mars acts through a transit, then by that act its force pours in upon the Native, and consequently, that transit is rightly judged to be dangerous in which the ASC, the significator of life, is determined to death by Mars, and in turn Mars, the *anaereta*, is determined by the ASC to life.

Similarly, because Mars constantly carries with it not only its own and essential virtue, but also that which it received from its radical determination, and it is indifferent to exercising the above said lethal force in the one or the other mode and in this or that kind of accident, such as actions, lawsuits, pleasures, etc. Consequently, when it transits through these significators by body or by harmful aspect, it is determined by individual things according to its mode or general signification, by which either death or danger to life can happen. And therefore when it transits through the ASC, it is determined to exerting lethal or sickening force, involving temperament, habits, or intelligence; [but] when it transits through the MC, involving actions, undertakings, or dignity, as happens to centurions leading their own soldiers to battle [as required] by duty, and thus with other [cases].

Chapter 7.
Whether the Transits of the Planets through the Places of the Revolutions should be Looked at.

We explain this, both by experience and by reason. By experience to be sure, since it will be proved below by many examples and observations that the Planets will transit through concordant places of the revolution on the days of their own effects. But by reason, since in revolutions the *Caelum* and the Planets are determined anew with respect to the native to the kinds of effects [indicated] by the houses of the significators in the figure, as we have said in Book 23, Chapter 6; and they are causes, partly by action and partly by potential, as in the nativity—namely, by the action of those things which are impressed celestially upon the native in the hour of the revolution, in which the Planets actively make their influxes; but by the potential of those things which by that very impression on the native himself will take place during the year or the month. But that which the *Caelum* and those Planets [represent] in potential in the revolution ought to be reduced to an action from a cause that is purely active, which is the transits of the Planets. Therefore, these too must be noted [as they move] through the principal places of the revolutions, but particularly in the revolution of the Sun. And especially on those days on which any directions of the revolutions are completed; but the transits through the places of the nativity are more effective.

Chapter 8.
Whether for the Production of all the Effects Happening to Men, the Transits Agreeing with the Planets, with their Directions and Revolutions are Necessary, and at what Time.

Of the effects or changes happening to a man, some are noteworthy which notably change the state of the native's body, mind, or fortune, such as marriage, a dangerous illness, a duel, etc; others are of small [consequence], such as anger, an entertainment, lack of self-control, etc.; but others are moderate, such as a lawsuit, a brief illness and recovery, etc., in all of which the facts of the condition and disposition of the native must be had. If in fact, for an armed robber stealing millions from the public, the theft of ten thousand might be thought a little thing; [but for one] established in the highest power near the King, those daily increments of fortune which happen are small, which would be great to a man of middle class status. Also, for someone prone [to be involved in] quarrels and duels, a duel will not in itself be a significant change; and the same logic applies to other things that are related to the Native's character or profession. But indeed for small changes, especially those concordant with character or profession, a transit alone can suffice; and that is frequently made known by experience; it is sufficient for those produced by a lighter cause; but produced by a great one it is alien to the analogy of cause and effect; and consequently, Venus transiting through the ASC of a voluptuous [person] can by her own nature alone provoke the Native to games, jokes, and entertainments, but more efficaciously if she were the ruler of the first or the fifth; and similarly, Mars transiting through the MC of a chivalrous soldier incites him to undertake some military action, especially [if it is] the ruler of the profession. More-over, moderate changes also require at least the agreement of a rev-olution; but great changes require in addition the concourse of a concordant direction. Besides, of the effects happening to a man, some are momentary, such as a fall, a wound, something unex-pected, a dignity unhoped-for and unexpectedly conferred; others are daily, such as a daily [attack of] fever, but [still] others lasting many days or months, such as an illness leading to death, a quarrel leading to a duel, a theft leading to the pillory, [or] love to marriage within days or after some months. Moreover, in these and in all other effects arising from the *Caelum*, concordant transits usually are present, as experience proves; therefore, it follows that they are necessary as a part of the celestial causes, just as the actual causes, without which also those potential causes of future effects in the radix and in a revolution are not reduced to an action.

Furthermore, in momentary and daily effects, the concordant transits are made on the very days of the effects if [while] not partile,[38] at least differing little from partility—to be sure, because the force of a transit is great near partility, but greatest when it is partile to the very degree. But in the effects [lasting] many days or months, since a notable change in the Native is not accomplished by celestial causes without the concurrence of an actual cause, concordant transits are necessary in the beginnings of these ef-fects; but it also often happens that there is a concordant transit at the end, such as on the day of death, of marriage, of the final re-ceipt of a dignity after many oppositions, etc.; and so this confirms and strengthens the previous transit at the beginning of the effect and completes its effect; but sometimes a single transit at the be-ginning suffices for the effect, on account of the strength of a benefic or the influx of a malefic that impels the Native to act or to suffer; and a concordant transit does not appear at the end, such as

---

[38] The Latin text has *si non partiles, saltem à partilitate parum differentes* 'if not partile, at least differing little from partility', which seems awkward at best. Per-haps we should simply delete *non* to yield the translation 'if partile [or] at least nearly partile'.

on the day of death resulting from a long illness. And this often deceives Astrologers with regard to the force of transits, when on the very day of death they see that no concordant transit is made, at least no notable one, for they are paying special attention to the day on which the effect is completed, when instead attention should be paid to the day on which it began; for that reason, you should not neglect the subsequent concordant transits for finding the day on which the effect will be finished or completed.[39]

Nevertheless, it should also be noted that transits at the beginning of revolutions are especially effective, namely, since they agree with the universal constitution, and this, to the degree allowed by the actual causes, they immediately reduce from potentiality to an act, so that there is no need for another actual cause, but especially in a revolution of the Moon. Therefore, that concordant transits are necessary for [the manifestation of] directions and revolutions, and especially for when [they manifest], is plain from what is said above.

Chapter 9.
For a given Direction Presaging a Significant Event, which Planet's Transit is more Necessary for the Production of the Effect, and through which Place, so that the Transit may be Said to be Concordant.

We shall attempt to unravel this burning question. It is certain that the effect of a direction occurs in that year in which it is completed if there is a concordant revolution; nevertheless, it cannot be done without an actual influx from a concordant transit; moreover, it is a question as to which Planet is appropriate to make a transit for the actual influx of the effect, whether it should be a significator, a promissor, or in fact some other? And then, through

---

[39] Morin seems to be saying that although sometimes only the beginning of a drawn-out event is indicated by a concordant transit, still the astrologer should look to see if there is a subsequent concordant transit that might indicate its end.

what place? Should it be the place of a significator, or a promissor, or in fact some other?

For which it should be noted: First. That any Planet in its own motion in the zodiac carries around both of its own virtues, namely an essential one from its own nature and an accidental one from its own determination with respect to the Native in the figure of his nativity—that is to say, a perpetually essential one, but an accidental one that it retains and maintains as long as that Native lives. Indeed, why not, because every Planet is determined to something with regard to individual men living in the whole world; it carries with it with respect to individuals that force to which it was determined with respect to each one in his radix, so long as that one lives, without any confusion of so many accidental virtues. Moreover, the bond of connection of each man with the celestial bodies through his natal constitution is dissolved by his death. And all of this is remarkable, if there is anything at all in universal nature that is remarkable, and very similar to God's method of working with regard to particulars.

Second. There are four principal places in the figure of the nativity in which there is the force to produce the effect of a direction, that is the places of the significator and the promissor of that direction, then the places of the rulers of both of those; but the significator is very often not a Planet, but a cusp, such as the ASC or the MC, to which it is not suitable to go, but to its ruler.

Third. Planets carrying their own force from their radical determination, almost always act according to that with respect to the Native, when an opportunity has been given in their own motion through a transit in concordant places of the figure. But sometimes they also act only in accordance with their own essential force; nevertheless, determined to the radical signification of the place through which the Planet itself is transiting, such as Venus through the MC, especially being free from the malefics, makes actions and undertakings fortunate, even if in the radix she had no particular signification of those things. And given that, any transiting

Planet becomes subordinate to the denotation of the promissor, namely because it is actively determined to the radical signification of the place through which it is transiting, and it acts in that regard because that is the denotation of the promissor.

Fourth. A planet under an actual influx by a transit excites either the native or the active and passive potentials of external causes to an effect.

With this understood, I say in general: a transit that agrees in signification with the direction is necessary for the effect of a direction [to occur]. That is, if the direction signifies an illness or a dignity, the transit [must] also signify an illness or a dignity. Moreover, the transit of a significator Planet through its own radical place by body or by an aspect concordant with the direction and powerful is in agreement; but more in agreement is the transit of that same [Planet] through the place of the promissor by body or by aspect, as [said] above; and similarly, the transit of the promissor Planet through its own radical place is in very strong agreement, but still more in agreement is its transit through the place of the significator. But when both the significator and the promissor are transiting their own radical places at the same time, or when they are in turn each in the other's place, or when they are together, or opposing or squaring [each other], or aspecting themselves by trine according to the quality of the direction, this is beyond doubt the strongest of all.

But since the significator in directions or its radical signification submits to the scheme of the subject, but the promissor submits to the scheme of the one driving the causes, and first is the transit through the significator, then through the promissor, because the latter follows, but the former precedes, it is especially made manifest that the Planet transiting through the significator, disposes the subject, at least by its act, to the power of the one acting; but transiting through the promissor, it excites the acting cause to the effect; if, therefore, the significator has transited through its own radical place, from its doubled determination of that same subject, radical namely, and due to the transit, the virtue of the significator with respect to that same subject will be doubled as will its disposition to the effect, which will burst forth from some internal cause of the subject, such as from the Native's own virtue, or debility, or temperament, etc.; whence, it is no wonder if in that year there is any notable direction of the Sun, either lucky or unlucky, on the very day of the revolution of the Sun, on which day the Sun transits through its own radical place, that a great good will happen for some, but for others a great evil, especially when the Sun is in an angle in that revolution and in a concordant site of the *Caelum*, just as is read about Emperor Charles V, for whom many notable instances of good luck happened on the days of his own revolutions.

Similarly, if the promissor transits through its own radical place, then from that its force and its radical signification is also doubled, both actually and potentially in the year in which the direction is actually made; and therefore the force of the acting cause will be doubled, which will be excited into action along with that transit; then generally on account of the strength of the one acting the effect is produced without any disposition of the subject, but from an external cause, as when one is killed or attains some dignity.

But when the significator transits through the place of the promissor or the other way around, both powers are increased and excited, namely the passive [power] of the subject and the active [power] of the one acting, because then each Planet is determined to their joint signification by its own transit; and consequently, the effect is accomplished more certainly and more efficaciously than before. However, the transit of the promissor through the place of the significator is the most effective of all for the strength of the agent and the production of the effect, because the promissor is determined twice towards the same action, namely by the direction and by the transit; [and] if there is added to those a concordant status of the promissor in the revolution, a major effect will follow. And it should be noted that when the significator transits the promissor, the subject exposes itself to the effectuation of the active cause. But on the contrary, when the promittor transits through

46

the place of the significator, the active cause applies itself to the subject, and it occasionally does that unexpectedly.

Minor effects are made when the promissor and the significator transit through the places of their own rulers or when those transit through the places of the promissor and the significator, unless the effect is directed from somewhere else; for since many [places] are always determined to the same thing, such as the ASC, its ruler, and the ruler of that ruler, etc., to life, the first cause is the most efficacious of all, the second less, the third still less, and the fourth of no efficacy—at least none perceptible—as I have already said. It should be noticed that the ruler of the promissor produces its changes, and similarly the ruler of the significator. But when the transits are not by body, but by the aspect of a Planet, the nature of the aspect must be considered and the house into which it falls, which the transiting Planet is moving through; for the effect will be a lucky or unlucky one, or one easy or difficult to be manifested in accordance with the nature of the aspect, and occasionally on account of the subject and the thing signified by that house. As if, Saturn, ruler of the eighth of the radix, came by direction to the Sun, the *apheta*, and transited through its square in the twelfth house, but [was] lethal, because Saturn is the *anaereta* by its own nature and by its determination on account of its rulership in the eighth.

Moreover, not only do the effects of a direction burst forth from the transit of a significator, a promissor, or the ruler of either one of these through some one of the 4 previously mentioned places, but also from their transit through other places concordant with the signification of the direction. As if the Moon, ruler of the ASC, is directed to a following Mars, but it has transited first through the place of the ASC or the Sun; or if the ASC itself is directed to Mars, and the ruler of the ASC has transited through the place of Saturn, ruler of the eighth, [then] illness and dangers to life are portended. Indeed, the effects of directions also emerge from the transits of other planets of a concordant signification through these same 4 places. As if the Sun, ruler of the tenth, is directed to Venus ruler of the second; but Jupiter, ruler of the ninth, has transited through the place of the Sun, honors and riches from an ecclesiastical dignity or from an ambassadorship are signified; for, the significations of riches, splendor, ecclesiastical dignity and ambassadorship are all related among themselves.

Moreover, in all transits attention must be paid to the Sun and the Moon, [which are] primary planets and more universal than the others, namely at what time the transits are made to the 4 above said places and to the transiting Planet; then, Jupiter and Venus must be taken into account for good effects, as well as Saturn and Mars for evil ones, having [considered] the scheme of the radical determination of the individual [Planets]. For from these the more prompt or stronger effects are produced. From which it is plain that the transits of the Planets can be concordant with the effect of a direction in multiple ways.

Chapter 10.
In which by many Examples and Observations the Virtue of Transits and their Actual Efficacy are Confirmed.

I could insert here innumerable observations most worthy of admiration relating to the virtue of transits made by me and by other Astrologers, both old and new. But because the nativities to which these pertain would also have to be supplied, it consequently seemed sufficient to defer a fuller proof to a particular book on the judgments of some selected nativities, which for the confirmation of the astrological theory that we have established, we have decided to judge by our method perhaps 100 [nativities], and to add them at the end of our *Astrological Prediction*, if GOD grants us [length of] life for this.[40]

---

[40] Unfortunately, this did not happen, for Morin died only a few years after writing these words (*Astrologiae nostrae practicae*, which I take to be the title of a book that he had in mind). He had also mentioned in one of the earlier books of the *Astrologia Gallica* that he had in mind to write a book on prediction.

And so, Gustavus Adolphus, King of Sweden, succumbed in the Battle of Lützen on 16 November 1632 at around 9 in the morning. and there was a direction of the radical MC to the 25th degree of Scorpio square Saturn from the eighth and to the body of Mars in the twelfth, then to the square of Jupiter ruler of the ASC from the second. Moreover, the direction of the MC in the solar revolution was at 29°40′ of Leo, the place of Mars in that same revolution, and square Saturn. And finally, the direction of the MC in the lunar revolution was again at 28 degrees of Leo in the eighth partilely square Saturn in that revolution. Therefore, there were those three directions in the worst houses of the figure and absolutely concordant for a violent death.

In fact, on the day of his death, Venus, ruler of the MC of the radix and of the solar revolution, which in the lunar revolution is found in the tenth in exile in Scorpio the domicile of Mars was transiting through the 9th degree of Sagittarius, close to the ASC of the radix and of the solar revolution, and partilely [conjunct] by its place in that revolution with [the fixed star] Cor Scorpionis.[41] And indeed, Saturn, the promissor in those revolutions, was in the 1st degree of Sagittarius, the place of Mars in the solar revolution, applying to the radical ASC of that revolution and conjunct Venus. Mars, moreover, was in the 19th degree of Sagittarius square the radical Moon, [and] applying to the place of the radical Sun, which, with the Moon, ruled the eighth of the radix and of the solar revolution, separating then from Venus. But the Sun, ruler of the eighth in the three aforesaid figures, and the *apheta* in the radix and in the solar revolution, was transiting through the 25th degree of Scorpio, partilely [conjunct] the radical place of Mars, and square Saturn and Jupiter in the radix itself; and in fact, Jupiter, ruler of the ASC of the radix and of the revolution in those same figures, was by transit in the 20th degree of Taurus, its own [place], and square the radical Saturn, and also opposite the radical place of Mars. All these transits, therefore, along with the figures and the

---

[41] Antares or α Centauri, which was in 4°38′ Sagittarius—close, but not partile.

directions, were very lethal; but the worst of all was the transit of the Sun, the *apheta*. And here, not only do the transits of the significator occur, namely Venus ruler of the MC, and Saturn with Mars, in their own squares and the body of the promissors, but others in agreement, as the Sun [being] the *apheta*, and Jupiter ruler of the ASC.

Constable Lesdiguières[42] began to be ill on 21 August 1626, when the New Moon occurred in 28 degrees of Leo. And therefore on that day the Moon was passing from the square of Mars and Saturn to the Sun; moreover, she was the ruler of the radical ASC and was being directed to her own sinister square, since she was the *apheta*, and with a quincunx to Saturn following.[43] And on the day of the beginning of his illness, Saturn, ruler of the eight in the radix and [also] in the solar revolution, was in 17 degrees of Virgo partilely opposite the radical Moon; but Mars, the ruler of Saturn, was in its place in the solar revolution; moreover, the Sun and the Moon were in trine to the radical Venus; but because she was the ruler of the twelfth in exile in Aries, she was not able to be of benefit, especially [acting] alone against the unlucky [aspects] mentioned above.

Moreover, he died on the 28th of September, when the Moon was in 5 degrees of Capricorn badly afflicted by the square to Mars and the Sun, [which were] conjoined in 5 degrees of Libra, the place of the Moon herself in the solar revolution. Venus, moreover, ruler of the twelfth of the radix, in the twelfth of the lunar revolution, was in 13 degrees of Scorpio, applying to the opposition of Mars and the place of Saturn [both] radical, which was sufficient for an old man, especially since in the last lunar revolution the Moon herself was very gravely afflicted by her opposition to the Sun and Saturn and to Mars almost partilely, from which the old man received a lethal impression in that month.

---

[42] The Latin text has his name as Disdiguieres, but it should be Lesdiguières, so I have changed it. He was François de Bonne, Duke of Lesdiguières (1543-1626), who was Constable of France from 1609.

[43] All the aspects in this sentence refer to primary directions in the natal chart.

Cardinal Richelieu, from an acute fever coming on top of a lengthy illness, from which he was not yet perfectly cured, at length died on the 4th of December 1642, when his radical ASC was directed to Jupiter in the eighth. And on that day, Venus, ruler of the twelfth, the ASC, and the eighth of the radix, was transiting through the 29th degree of Capricorn square the ASC itself, and also Jupiter was transiting through the 11th degree of Pisces square its own radical [place]; and these [were the aspects] of the significator and the promissor. And in addition in the solar revolution, the Moon, Saturn, and Jupiter were conjoined in the seventh opposite the Sun; but in the revolution of the Moon, Saturn, Jupiter, and the Moon were conjoined in the eighth in square to the Sun and Mercury, rulers of the eighth of the radix; and Saturn was partilely conjunct the Moon, which is very bad for the life in revolutions of the Moon, but it was even worse than that because that kind of conjunction was in the eighth, with the Moon being ruler of the twelfth. Besides, Mars, ruler of the first of the radix was on the very day of his death in 2 Taurus, his own radical opposition; and Mercury, ruler of the eighth of the radix, had returned to its own radical place partilely; and Saturn was in the place of the radical Moon partilely. Therefore, by so many cruelly conspiring celestial causes he was overwhelmed, who thought that he could succumb to nothing terrestrial. But here, not only do the transits concordant with the significator and the promissor concur, which are Venus and Jupiter, but also the transits concordant with the other Planets—namely those which were the significators of life and death, by nature or by determination or by both.

Lord Tronson began to become ill on the 2nd of October 1642, on which day the direction of the radical ASC was to the sinister square of the Sun; moreover, on that same day, Venus, ruler of the ASC and the eighth, was on the cusp of the second of the radix, and Mars was on the cusp of the eighth, partilely opposite, and square to the radical place of the Moon, which was then in opposition to the radical Mars, and the latter was opposed in the revolution of the Sun, but in the revolution of the Moon that immediately preceded his illness, it was square to the Moon, and Saturn was opposed to the Sun, [both of] which were very bad; moreover, he died on the 8th of December, on which day Venus in the 2nd degree of Aquarius and Mars in the 2nd degree of Taurus were partilely square, which must be particularly noted; and again, the Moon was applying to the opposition of the radical Mars; and the Sun was in the 17th degree of Sagittarius applying to the radical place of Saturn; and then its square was debilitated; all of which things were very bad and threatening death.

The Blessed Father Charles de Condren was made Sub-Deacon on the 24th of May 1613, in which year the Sun in the first was directed to the 17th degree of Capricorn, sinister trine to Jupiter, ruler of the ASC in the ninth. And on that day, the Sun, ruler of the tenth, along with the Moon in the revolution of the Sun, was transiting through the 4th degree of Gemini trine the radical MC and the Moon in that revolution, which was in the 5th degree of Libra, in the place of the MC; but Jupiter was in its own radical place partilely. And its ruler Mercury was in the 23rd degree of Gemini opposite the radical Sun; moreover, Venus, ruler of the MC, was in the 17th degree of Taurus in partile trine to Jupiter itself; therefore, all these transits were notable and concordant with an ecclesiastical dignity.

Moreover, on the following 17th of September he was made a Deacon. And then the Sun was in the 25th degree of Virgo in the ninth, partilely square its own radical place, [and] Jupiter, ruler of the Sun, was in the MC of the radix; but Venus, ruler of that MC, was in the radical place of Mars in the tenth, which she was ruling; consequently, these transits were outstandingly concordant.

In the year 1614 on the 17th of September he was made a Priest, on which day the Sun that was in the first of the radix, and Mercury, ruler of Jupiter in the ninth in the radix, were partilely conjoined in the ninth house in partile square to the Sun; moreover, the Moon was transiting Jupiter and their opposition; and these [configurations] were greatly concordant.

In the year 1617 on the 17th of June, he applied to enter into the Congregation of the Oratory of Jesus, in which year Mars in the tenth of the radix was directed to Venus, its ruler; and on that very day it was in the 15th degree of Virgo in the radical place of Jupiter, and the Sun was in the 26th degree of Gemini in its own radical square.

In the year 1642 on the 6th of January, the holy man died venerably around 6 AM, in which year the Sun, the *apheta* in the first house, was directed to the sinister square of the Moon who was in the twelfth afflicted by the opposition to Saturn. Moreover, he began to become ill on the 29th of December 1641, on which day the Moon herself was transiting through the ASC, and Mars [was transiting] partilely through the place of the radical Moon, and Saturn in the eighth degree of Pisces was square the radical ASC. Moreover, on the day of his death, Saturn was in partile square to the radical ASC. And Mars, ruler of the Moon, was in the 6th degree of Sagittarius nearly on that radical ASC; and finally, the Moon was in opposition to the radical Jupiter, ruler of the ASC; all of which were portending his demise on that very day, as we had foretold.

In the year 1605 on the 9th of July at about eight in the evening I was wounded on account of a woman. Then in fact the radical ASC was directed to the sinister square of Venus, followed by a square to the Sun, ruler of the fifth, and Jupiter, ruler of the eighth, with which Venus herself was conjoined. And on that day, Mars, ruler of the radical ASC; Venus, ruler of the first; the Sun, ruler of the fifth; and Mercury, ruler of the sixth, were conjoined in the radical place of Mars, and trine the radical Saturn, ruler of the MC in the twelfth; but Saturn itself was transiting through the eighth house of the radix [and] square the radical Moon, by which everything was agreeing with the effect and its circumstances and with the sublunar causes.

In the year 1612 on the 30th of May, I was seized by a severe and lengthy illness. Then, moreover, the ASC was directed conversely to the Moon and Jupiter, significators of illnesses and death; but directly, they were directed to the 9th degree of Gemini, not far from the square to Saturn. Moreover, on that same day there was a great eclipse of the Sun in that very degree, and the Sun and the Moon were significators of illnesses in the nativity, and Saturn, also a principal significator of illnesses, was in the radical place of the Moon, to which it was also partilely conjoined in the preceding revolution of the Moon; and this was very bad and lethal or at least very dangerous, as has already been remarked many times above. But Mars, ruler of the radical ASC, was in the 6th degree of Aries in the twelfth square his own radical place; and Jupiter, ruler of the eighth, was partilely in his own place in the revolution of the Sun in the fifth. By these, therefore, there was excited an illness [that was] severe, lengthy, and one in which hope for life had been given up by the physicians.

In the year 1613 on the 9th of May, I achieved the Doctorate in Medicine, in which year the MC was directed to the square of the Part of Fortune and the partile semi-sextile of Saturn, ruler of the MC, and Saturn itself was directed to the Part of Fortune. In addition, moreover, the ASC was conversely directed to the Moon as well as to Jupiter, ruler of the Sun and Saturn, which [latter] presided over the MC.

Moreover, on the very day of the effect, Jupiter was in opposition to the radical Moon and trine the MC; the Sun was in the first of the radix in sextile to the radical Moon and trine the MC, in which the Moon was then; and consequently, the Sun, Moon, and Jupiter were in trine among themselves by syzygy; Saturn, moreover, was in partile semi-sextile to the ASC; and Venus, ruler of the Part of Fortune, was in the 29th degree of Aries near the radical ASC.

In the year 1615 on the 7th of July, I fell into the danger of a violent death from a missile thrown at me from [a distance of] three paces in the Rhine, in which I was swimming for pleasure; in which year, the radical ASC was directed directly to the square of

Saturn in the ecliptic and conversely to Venus. Moreover, on the evening of that same day, Mars, ruler of the ASC, was in the 10th degree of Virgo almost opposite Saturn, and Saturn was in the 27th degree of Aries [conjunct] the radical ASC. Venus, moreover, was in the 17th degree of Leo quincunx the Moon [being placed] in the 5th house where the quincunxes of Venus, the Sun, Jupiter, Saturn, and the Moon fell. From these things, and because the Sun, ruler of the fifth is in the twelfth with Saturn and Jupiter, ruler of the eighth, pleasures were almost always dangerous for me with respect to my life or my health. And finally, the Moon was on the cusp of the eighth with [the fixed star] Cor Scorpii;[44] the transits were therefore very bad.

In the year 1616 on the 1st of January, I underwent another frightful danger from a fall from my horse from a high place and submersion [in the river below]. On which day, Mars, ruler of the radical ASC, and the Sun were conjoined in opposition to the radical Mars near the MC; the Moon was in Gemini square the radical Saturn and Moon; Jupiter and Venus were in the eighth of the radix in another square to Saturn and Moon in the radix, and consequently opposed to that Moon by syzygy.

In that same year 1616 on the 16th of April, I fell into a severe and malign illness, at which time the ASC was directed to the square of Saturn with latitude.[45] Moreover, on that very day, the Sun, Moon, and Saturn were transiting through the ASC itself. Mars, ruler of the ASC, was in the 6th degree of Aries square its own radical place, as [it was] on the 30th of May 1612, on which day I fell into another very malign illness that was mentioned above. Moreover, Venus was in the 16th degree of Pisces, the place of the radical Moon and Saturn.

In the year 1629, I was made Regius Professor of Mathematics through the assistance of friends. In which year, the MC was di-

---

[44] The fixed star Antares or α Scorpii, which was at 4°24′ Sagittarius.

[45] That is, a *mundane* square or a square *in mundo* as it is usually said.

rected to Mercury, ruler of the second, in the eleventh. I took up the post on the 30th of June, on which [day] Saturn, ruler of the MC, was in its own antiscion and exaltation with Spica Virginis;[46] Mars, ruler of the radical ASC, was in the 10th degree of Taurus, the place of the Part of Fortune; the Sun was in the 9th degree of Cancer, the place of the radical Mars; Venus, ruler of the first and of the Part of Fortune, was in the 4th degree of Cancer trine her own radical [place] and the Sun and Jupiter, [and] near the place of Mars. Moreover, the Moon was in the 12th degree of Scorpio in the seventh trine the radical Saturn and Moon; and the undertaking turned out very fortunately. Moreover, I received letters [authorizing] my dignity stamped with the royal seal on the following 3rd of August, on which [day] Saturn was as above; Mars, ruler of the MC in the revolution of the Sun, was in the 4th degree of Gemini square the radical Sun and Jupiter; and Mercury was in opposition to the radical Sun and Jupiter.

In the year 1634 on the 30th of March, I gave a public demonstration of the Science of Longitudes. And then the MC was directed to the Sun. Moreover, on that same day, Saturn, ruler of the MC, was in 21 Sagittarius opposite Jupiter in the revolution of the Sun, and Jupiter was in 24 Gemini opposite that same Saturn and almost in the antiscion of the radical Mars; but that Mars, potent because of its exaltation in the MC of the radix, was in the 13th degree of Virgo opposite the radical Saturn and trine the radical MC; and in fact the Sun and Mercury were in the 10th degree of Aries square the radical Mars; and finally, the Moon was in the radical ASC. And indeed all the astronomers testified that that Science was perfectly demonstrated. But Cardinal Richelieu, with the treachery and betrayal of my Commissioners, wickedly defrauded me of the promised prize, which the opposition and squares in the above mentioned transits foreshadowed.

In the year 1642 on the 2nd of November, I was seized by a lengthy and difficult illness from the direction of the ASC to Mars

---

[46] The fixed star Spica or α Virginis was at 18°40′ Libra and Saturn was at 16°51′ Libra (or at 16°44′ Libra according to the *Rudolphine Tables*).

in the ecliptic.[47] And on that day began a revolution of my Moon, in the figure of which the opposition of the radical Mars was ascending; and Saturn, ruler of the ASC, was almost partilely conjoined to the Moon in the second house, for the Moon is applying to Saturn, whom she overtook within two hours, at which time the illness was beginning, even though imperceptibly, for it was only at about 3 PM that it broke out perceptibly by a rigor. But the Moon in the figure of her own revolution conjoined or opposed to Saturn we have already very often said to be very unlucky—how much more so then with an illness beginning? Here, unless I am mistaken, it was caused by that conjunction.

Chapter 11.
[Determining] the Exact Time of Events by a Transit, and Whether their Latitude should be Observed. The Doctrine Confirmed by Celestial Charts.

The highest crown of judicial Astrology, from which the greater admiration of this science and the more honored fame of the astrologer arises is to predict the exact time of events to the day and the hour, which has happened many times not only to me but also to older Astrologers, as is witnessed by History; and it will be much more familiar to those of latter days because of the universality of Astrology, but especially on account of that doctrine of directions and revolutions and also transits already set forth more precisely and accurately than it ever was before. Moreover, that time can be conjectured by a variety of ways and can become known as follows.

First, therefore, when the promissor of the direction and the planet that is the significator return to their own radical locations in the year in which the direction is completed, or one of them transits through the place of the other by body or by a concordant aspect, or both of them are conjoined in another place, then the effect is de-

---

[47] That is a conjunction *in zodiaco* as it is usually said.

pending upon that sort of transit of theirs; for then the force of their radical determination and its virtue are doubled. Indeed, all the planets, when they transits their own opposition or square in the radix, excite their own radical signification to actuality, on account of the force of that cross in the sky, which Johannes Francus Offusius writing *Against Astrology*[48] was unable not to admire and acknowledge.

Second. If any planet is transiting partilely through the place of another, [and] it should happen that both, by conjunction or by concordant strong aspect, are joined together by syzygies, or at least the transiting planet is connected with the ruler of the house through which it is transiting, then the effect will be produced by such a transit, if it agrees with a direction, for thus the significator and the promissor aid and excite each other.

Third. If to a direction of the radical ASC to the body, the square, or the opposition of Saturn, especially when it is the ruler of the eighth or twelfth house, there is added in that same year a transit of that same Saturn through the ASC, by its square, or opposition, but especially by a bodily transit, illness or some danger to the life is certainly to be feared; but especially if to the transit of Saturn there is added a transit of Mars to the lights in the sixth, the eighth, or the twelfth aspecting the powers adversely, or is joined with them bodily. For then the ASC is very badly afflicted, and [also] the Native because of the actual influx of the malefics affecting his life. And there is the same logic with the others, for here and elsewhere we very often set forth a universal doctrine from a particular case.

Fourth. When a benefic planet is in the MC of the radix or the ruler of the MC itself is well posited, and in a concordant direction

---

[48] Probably a reference to the book *De divina astrorum facultate in larvatam astrologiam* (Paris, 1570) 'On the Divine Power of the Stars Against a Bewitched Astrology'. See Thorndike, HMES 6, pp. 22-24,108-111. Offusius (c. 1500-c. 1565) was a medical doctor who had devised a new system of astrology, and, as usual, denounced other astrologers who were using traditional systems. Thorndike gives some details.

and revolution that same planet transits through the ASC of the radix, or the place of the ruler of the ASC well disposed and very well configured with that ruler, then some good fortune will come to the Native in his undertakings or in dignities; for to these [accidents] the MC as well as the ASC are determined together in the act, or rather the Native is determined by the ASC and the MC. And the same logic applies to other things.

Fifth. The status of the Native must be considered, while the direction and the revolution are in effect, agreeing in a lucky or an unlucky accident, [and] strong concordant transits are present. For if someone has a quarrel leading to a duel, in the year of a menacing direction and revolution, and there is a malefic in the eighth of the radix, at the time when the ruler of the ASC of the radix transits the place of that malefic or its opposition, a duel will take place and he will be killed, unless, conscious of the danger, he avoids it, having prudently overcome a proclivity of his nature. And the same logic applies to other things.

Sixth. In the transit of the planets through the radical places, it must be seen to what the transiting planets and the place through which they are transiting are determined in the radix. For if both of them are determined to the same kind of good thing, as when the two benefics are in the first or the tenth, or they are determined to good things of different kinds, such as the ruler of the ASC and the ruler of the second or the MC, then the transit of one of them through the place of the other by body or by benefic aspect will be opportune for a fortunate effect; just as when the Sun in the tenth of the radix transits the place of Jupiter in the first by body or by trine; but if they were determined to some kind of evil, as two planets in the eighth or the twelfth, especially malefics, or to evils of different kinds, as the ruler of the eighth and the ruler of the twelfth or one of them to good and the other to evil, then the transit of one of the malefics through the place of the other by body or by aspect will be opportune for a bad effect; moreover, a transit by a benefic aspect will [still] be unsafe, because Planets determined to evils very often harm more than the benefic aspects help, especially those [Planets] that are malefic by nature; as on the contrary, Jupiter and Venus determined to good things, also help by square or opposition, although not without some difficulty. And the [very] days of the events of the aforesaid things and others like them can be foreseen.

Seventh. For effects [to eventuate] from transits, not only is it required that the transits of the Planets are made conformably in the *Caelum*, but also that they are made in a concordant location with respect to the horizon and the Native, for only then do they produce their effects; and from them the [very] hour of the accidents can be discovered. As the transit of Saturn through the degree of the ASC must be feared, especially in that same hour in which Saturn rises with that degree in the horizon that the Native is then occupying, and its transit through the MC, in which hour Saturn will be in the middle of the *Caelum*; and [also] its transit through the place of the Sun, in which hour Saturn is in the circle of position of the radical Sun; and that hour must also be feared in which Saturn is in the opposite locations; because indeed it must be particularly understood about the things signified by those places of Saturn from the contrary radical determination. For not only must Saturn's transit through the degree of the radical ASC be feared, when by its daily motion it will be in the rising point of the horizon, but also when with that same motion it will transit the spaces of the first, seventh, eighth, and twelfth houses, which are inimical to life. And the reasoning is the same about other transits, good as well as bad, by body or by a concordant aspect.

And from this the reason can be found why the transits of the Moon, even though they are the most frequent, are nevertheless rarely effective; namely because on account of the swift motion of the Moon it can rarely happen that when it transits through the place of Saturn, the *Primum Caelum* is at the Native's horizon,[49] as at the hour of his nativity.

---

[49] The text has *ad Horizontem vel Natum* 'at the horizon or the Native', which doesn't make sense. I suppose it should read *ad Horizontem Nati* 'at the Native's horizon' or something of the sort.

And because this mode is one of the principal ones for discovering the hour of the effect, from those[50] observations which we can offer for the common good, it is pleasing to add here some examples of it with respect to the natal figures, the revolutions of which are given in Book 23. And the times of those effects were known to us down to the hour. For thus, with regard to these same figures displayed by virtue of the directions, revolutions, and transits, the truth of the doctrine established by us will be shown more evidently than it is permitted to anyone to be experienced in [the writings of] others here and there.

Therefore, Gustavus Adolphus, King of Sweden began a battle against the Imperial forces around 9 A.M. on the 16th of November 1632, and in the beginning of that encounter he was killed. Moreover, the figure of the *Caelum* was then as shown below.

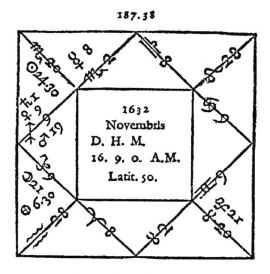

Figure of the King's Death
16 November 1632
9:00 AM LAT

---

[50] There is an illegible word (*loco*?) in the Latin text. I have assumed that it should read *illis* 'those'.

In fact, the *Caelum* is disposed as it is in the nativity, the revolution of the Sun, and nearly as in the revolution of the Moon, which is most worthy of note. Venus, ruler of the MC, the significator in a lethal direction, was in the ASC, the primary significator of life, with a violent fixed star,[51] besieged by Saturn and Mars, the *anaeretas* in this direction, which three planets were rising in that very hour, with Mars applying to the radical place of the Sun ruler of the eighth, being partilely in the place of the radical Mars and square the radical Saturn in the twelfth house, opposed to Jupiter, ruler of the ASC, Saturn, Venus, and Mars; moreover, the Moon, ruler of the eighth, was in exile in partile trine to Jupiter and opposite the eighth. Therefore, such an hour was very bad, and it was portending a lethal warlike action or undertaking, on the day on which lethal transits were being made.

Cardinal Richelieu passed away on the 4th of December 1642 around noon; and the figure was such as this.

250. 30.

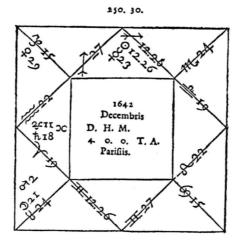

Cardinal Richelieu's Death
4 December 1642
noon LAT

---

[51] Antares or α Scorpii, which was at 4°38′ Sagittarius.

In which the ASC is opposite the ASC of the revolution of the Moon; and the radical ASC, the significator in a lethal direction, was in the eighth in square to Venus, its own ruler, from the twelfth, which in this figure was ruler of the eighth along with Mars,[52] to whose square she was applying; moreover, Jupiter, the promissor and *anaereta* by its own opposition, was in the first in its own radical square, and conjunct Saturn, ruler of the twelfth and the ASC, in square to the Sun and Mercury, rulers of the eighth of the radix, which was then with the Sun in his own radical square; but Mars, significator of life in the nativity,[53] was transiting through its own opposition, in exile and along with the Moon opposed to the eighth, [both of] which [planets] Venus ruled from the twelfth; therefore, all the planets agreed on the death of this person at that hour.

The Blessed Father Charles de Condren, died on the first day of January in the year 1641, at around 6 AM; and the figure of the *Caelum* was then like that shown on the next page.

In which the *Caelum* is disposed as in the nativity and the revolution of the Moon; the Sun, the significator in a lethal direction, is ruler of the eighth in the first afflicted by the square of Mars, ruler of the twelfth of the radix and of this figure, transiting through its own radical opposition; moreover, the Moon square its own *anaereta* is found in the eighth afflicted by the opposition of Saturn, [which] is in partile sinister square to the radical Moon. Therefore, the transits and the situation of the Planets at that hour were very bad.

The very noble Lord Tronson, a great friend of the Reverend Father, died on the 8th of December 1642 at around 9 AM under a figure of this sort:

---

[52] Because parts of both Libra and Scorpio are included in the eighth house.

[53] Richelieu's chart as drawn by Morin has the 30th degree of Libra rising, so the first house consists mainly of Scorpio, whence Morin considers Mars to be the ruler of the first house.

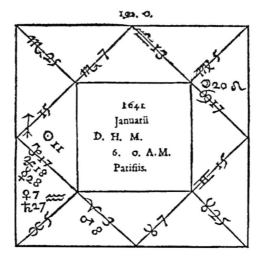

Father Charles de Condren's Death
1 January 1641
6 AM LAT

209. 0.

1642
Decembris
D. H. M.
8. 9. 0. T.A.
Patifiis.

Death of Lord Tronson
8 December 1642
9:00 AM LAT

In which Venus, ruler of the ASC and the eighth of the radix, and consequently the significator of a lethal direction, is found in the first afflicted by a square of Mars. But the Sun, the promissor, and in this figure ruler of the eighth, is found in the twelfth with Mercury, ruler of the eighth of the radix, which is transiting through the radical place of Saturn; and both of them are afflicted by the square of Saturn, ruler of the ASC, which is in the second with Jupiter, ruler of the twelfth, the Sun, and Mercury; therefore, there were such transits and situations of the Planets hostile to life, since even the Moon would then kill.

I myself received a very dangerous wound on the 9th day of July in 1605 at around 8:24 in the evening, and the figure was like the following.

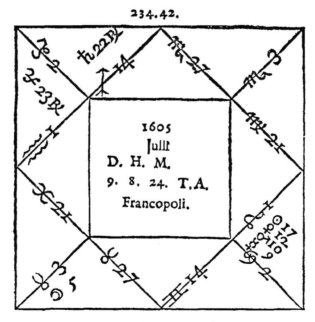

Morin Dangerously Wounded
9 July 1605
8:24 PM LAT

In which the ASC of the radix, significator of the direction, is opposite the eighth,[54] and the opposition of the fifth cusp is ascending;[55] moreover, Venus, the promissor square her own [position], is in the sixth applying to the Sun, ruler of the fifth of the radix, and conjunct Mars and Mercury above the place of the radical Mars, opposite the MC, and Mercury, ruler of the second and the sixth of the radix, opposed to the fifth of the radix. But here, Mercury is ruler of the fifth and the eighth applying to Mars, ruler of the MC; and there are Mercury conjunct Venus and the Sun in opposition to Jupiter, rulers of the eight of the radix, cadent and retrograde in the twelfth. and finally, Saturn is in the eighth of the radix, here opposed to the fifth. Therefore, the transits and the situation of the Planets were threatening death from the things signified by the fifth because of a woman. But God took pity upon me; and to Him go my eternal rendering of thanks.

On the 7th day of July in 1615 around 10:20 in the evening, I underwent the greatest danger of dying and drowning in the Rhine; and the figure was as follows on the next page.

In which, the ASC, significator in the bad direction of that year, is found in the first house, and Saturn, promissor by its square, is transiting through the ASC itself; and the radical place of Saturn is ascending in a water sign, to which Mars, ruler of the radical ASC is partilely opposed. Moreover, Jupiter, ruler of the ASC, is in the eighth also in a water sign under the rulership of Mars in trine to the Sun and Mercury from the fifth, separating from the radical place of Mars, also in a water sign. And the Moon, ruler of the Sun and Mercury, is in the eighth with the [the fixed star] Cor Scorpii.[56] Finally, Venus, ruler of the radical first, is found in the

---

[54] Morin's ASC degree was in 28 Aries; in the chart dawn above Libra is intercepted in the 8th house; consequently the opposition of his ASC degree does fall in the 8th.

[55] The 5th cusp of Morin's natal chart was in 2 Leo, and its opposition 2 Aquarius is in fact rising in the chart shown.

[56] The fixed star Antares or α Scorpii, which was at 4°24′ Sagittarius.

260. 20.

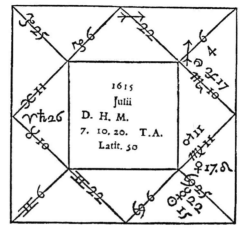

Morin's Near Drowning
7 Jul 1615
10:20 PM LAT

311. 33.

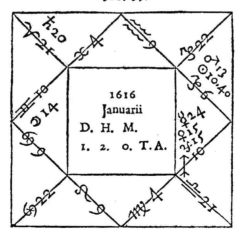

Morin Fell From His Horse
1 January 1616
2 PM LAT

67

fifth of the radix and the sixth of this figure in square to Jupiter, ruler of the eighth of the radix in the eighth of this figure; therefore, everything was very bad by situation and determination. Praise be to God! Amen.

On the 1st of January 1616 at around 2 PM I underwent a terrible, near fatal danger from a fall from my horse from a precipice and [subsequent] submersion, and the figure was thus [shown on previous page].

In which the ASC, then the significator of an active and threatening direction, was in the twelfth of this figure, to which Saturn, the promissor, was applying by its own square, [which] in this figure was the ruler of the eighth; Mars, moreover, ruler of the radical ASC itself, was then in the eighth with the Sun on an opposition to the radical Mars, and this in square to Saturn badly afflicted by sign and house. The ASC of this figure was in sinister square to the radical Saturn, in which the Moon is found opposed to Jupiter, ruler of the eighth of the radix, also transiting that house. All of which things corresponded to a great danger; and because I experienced that danger due to the malevolence of a fortune-teller, it must also be acknowledged that the Devil took careful note of the opportunity from the hours of the stars, and to accommodate craftily[57] his own perverse arts for the destruction of men to the natural fate that he cannot overrule. But with God's supreme pity and the most faithful guardianship of my Good Angel, I was in short miraculously freed [from that danger], for which my soul will praise the Lord eternally. Amen!

On the 2nd of November 1642 around noon I was seized by a fever along with a rigor, from which [there resulted] a long and difficult illness; and the figure was like this.[58]

---

[57] It seems to me that we should read *callide* 'craftily' rather than *calide* 'immediately', and I have so translated it.

[58] In the text, the figure is rotated counter-clockwise by 90°, but I have restored it to its proper orientation.

In which there ascended the places of Saturn and the Moon of the radix; and the Moon and Saturn were significators of illnesses in the nativity, here partilely conjunct, and moreover platically

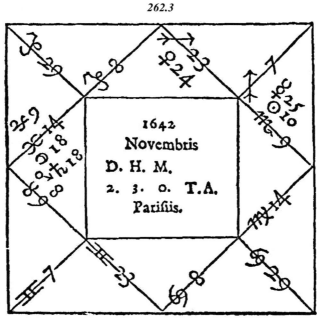

Morin Struck by a Fever
2 November 1642
3 PM LAT

conjoined to the ASC and to Jupiter, ruler of the eighth of the radix. The revolution of the Moon had only preceded [this time] by about two hours. And in fact Mars, ruler of the first, was in exile on the cusp of the second and opposite the Sun in the eighth, whom Mars himself ruled. And the Sun and Jupiter were in trine aspect but harmful on account of their determination to illnesses and death. Therefore, these circumstances and the situation of the Planets was unlucky and consistent with illness.

And these [examples] of the exact time of events [deduced]

from transits is sufficient; for from these, all the rest of the things pertaining to this subject can be easily understood and deduced.

But what consideration should we give to the latitude of the transiting Planets, I say there is not much necessity to observe it, at least in the case of the lighter Planets, whose transits are swift. especially because if the directions to the degrees of longitude of the promissors are very often valid, as was plain from the foregoing, why not also the transits, when it is not necessary for the effect that they be partile? Nevertheless, the more partilely the transits are made, the more effective they will be; and the less partile, the weaker. Consequently, if Mars with southern latitude of 3 degrees transits the opposition to the Moon with a northern latitude of 5 degrees, such a transit will be of little virtue; and to one that is beyond the orb of virtue of the Planets, there is no noticeable virtue.[59]

Chapter 12.
Whether the Planets act upon the Native through their own Syzygies Outside of the Places of the Nativity through which their Transits are Customarily Made. And How and When.

By transiting through the places of the nativity, the Planets not only produce effects upon the Native or upon things pertaining to him in accordance with their own radical determination, as was said above but they also act through their mutual syzygies[60] outside of those places or in empty houses of the figure—not, however, outside of that determination, but in accordance with it. For example, on that day on which the ruler of the ASC and the ruler of the 8th are conjoined— even in empty houses of the figure—an illness or a danger to life will occur. Similarly, on that day on which the ruler of the ASC and the ruler of the MC are

---

[59] Here Morin is applying orbs to distance in *latitude*.
[60] That is, through their conjunctions.

conjoined or are in trine aspect, some good fortune will happen for the Native in his undertakings, actions, or honors.

Besides, effects do not always follow from these syzygies, but only when they make good the lack of transits, namely if two things are perceived in them by which they are rendered effective. First, that the planets constituting the syzygy are badly configured and disposed to an evil effect presignified by the directions and the revolutions, or[61] favorably for good. Second, that they are made in the house or houses of the radical figure concordant with the effect. If indeed the Planets act through their syzygies, in accordance with the house or houses of the radical figure in which the syzygy happens, and the nature or quality of the syzygies. Moreover, the effect of the syzygy happens on the very day of the syzygy and often at the very hour; that is, if at that [time] the Planets constituting the syzygy and rotated by the diurnal motion are found in a concordant situation with respect to the horizon—that is, in concordant houses of the celestial figure that is then erected. Moreover, the reason why such syzygies are effective and how is this: because the bodies themselves of the Planets are causes of the celestial places in the figure of the radix, since they are determined by those very Planets whose places they are said to be. And the Planets themselves were also determined in the radix to this or that kind of accident for the Native according to their own situation in the figure, [by their] corporeal [position] and rulership; and they retain their own force on the Native from such a determination, and they continue to carry that same efficacy on the Native as long as he lives, as we said in Chapter 4. Consequently, it results from this that when the rulers of the ASC and the eighth come together by syzygy—even outside the radical places—they nevertheless act upon the Native himself in accordance with [the nature of] that syzygy and its radical determination, for it is proper that both of them concur for the effect [to take place].

---

[61] The Latin text has *& fauste pro bono* 'and favorabty for good', but the *&* must be a typographical error for *aut* 'or'.

Chapter 13.
The Aphorisms or Principal Laws of Transits.

One who is strong in the theory of Astrology can compose innumerable particular aphorisms because particulars depend upon the universals already known from theory. We, therefore, shall only put here some principal universal aphorisms, from the knowledge of which other aphorisms both universal and particular pertaining to transits may easily be deduced. Therefore, let it be that:

First. The transits of Saturn, Jupiter, and Mars are more efficacious than the transits of the other planets. For these, being slower than the others, stay longer in the places through which they transit, especially if they are stationary; and consequently from these places they make a more efficacious actual impression on the Native. And hence it follows that the transits of the Moon (at least the solitary ones) are of the least virtue of all; for otherwise their effects would be the most frequent, contrary to experience, but [those] of Saturn are the greatest of all, especially the stationary or retrograde ones.

2. The effect of any transit arises from the actual combination of the radical significations of the transiting Planet and of the place through which it transits, having taken into account the nature and analogy of the Planets.

3. The transits of the Planets outside of the places of the nativity, namely the 12 cusps, the 7 Planets, the Part of Fortune, and their aspects and antiscions, are of no efficacy with regard to the Native. For, as the essence of the Native depends upon these [places], so also do all his changes. And yet, the syzygies of the Planets in empty houses of the figure are effective, as we have said in Chapter 12.

4. In [evaluating] transits, the bodily place of the transiting Planet must be noted. For Mars transiting over the cusp of the 7th in opposition to the ASC more certainly portends lawsuits by reason of its bodily position than illness by reason of its opposition to the ASC.

5. In every transit, the celestial state of the transiting Planet must be noted at the time in which it is transiting—namely, whether it agrees with or is contrary to the effect signified by the Planet. For the energy of the transiting Planet is increased or diminished by that. And its radical latitude and that of the transit must be noted.

6. During an effect caused by the stars through directions and transits, the motion of the Moon and of those Planets that are being judged because of that effect must be diligently observed and how in the radical figure they may be moved by transits from place to place of similar or dissimilar signification; then too, how by their own motion they apply by syzygies to the lights and the Planets of similar or dissimilar signification either by [their] nature or by [their] determination. For from this the success and end [result] of the effects can be discovered.

7. The transits of the Moon through the places of a figure erected for the beginning of an illness, but especially through its own square and opposition, are of great virtue, as is established by experience, and it will be shown, when in the *Practice of Astrology*[62] (If GOD grants us time for this [purpose]) we will treat of the use of Astrology in Medicine. Why then, in a figure erected for the beginning of any other thing, at any time during [its occurrence], will the transits through the places of that figure by the Moon and the other Planets that signify that thing not be effective? And this to be sure is of use in the doctrine of elections; but if the figure of the nativity is at hand, the scheme of that figure will have to be especially considered in [judging] transits.

8. Since all the Planets act by direction as well as by transit in accordance with their own radical determination and their own nature, and in the nativity they are determined to some particular thing, such as life, or to its opposite, such as illnesses and death, or

---

[62] This is the title of a book that Morin intended to write, but which unfortunately he did not live to write.

neither to life nor to death, but to some other thing, such as dignities; therefore, in directions and in transits, a promissor Planet determined to life and a benefic and well disposed coming to the significators of life, but especially the ASC, strengthens the life; [but] determined to the contrary, it harms the life, or it destroys it; but, determined to neither of these, it neither helps nor harms, or it does nothing (at least, nothing significant) affecting the life. Similarly, a Planet transiting through the MC suited to honors by its nature and radical determination, will confer honors; but determined to the contrary, such as to prisons, exile, [or] death, especially when it is malefic by nature and badly disposed or inimical to the MC, will destroy those same things, or it will harm them very much, or it will impede their occurrence; but when it is determined to neither of these, it will cause nothing (or at least nothing significant) regarding honors, actions, or undertakings, although it can occasion some accident lightly affecting them in accordance with its own nature or its radical determination—indeed, to confer or destroy a dignity is a greater effect than to introduce some trivial good or evil accident to [an existing] dignity. But major effects result from greater causes, and minor effects from minor causes, which are those not determined to any particular thing. And that same reasoning applies to other things.

9. In transits, not otherwise than in directions, the more ways a Planet coming to the MC is determined to honors, and is in better state, both in the radix as well as at the time of the direction and especially at the time of the transit, the more efficaciously and abundantly it will bring good fortune to the Native in his undertakings and actions. Just as, if the Sun or Jupiter is the ruler of the MC in the radix, and at an age concordant with dignities, it is directed as promissor to the MC, [and] on that day of the year in which the direction is completed, it will transit that same MC [while it is] well disposed by body or by aspect, especially with a concordant revolution, it will cause some notable good fortune in dignities or undertakings, since it is determined to honors in multiple ways, that is by nature or analogy, rulership, direction and by a concordant

transit, with a fortunate state. But on the contrary, the more ways that a Planet transiting the MC is determined against honors, the more efficaciously will it bring bad fortune to the Native in connection with honors and undertakings; as for example, Saturn in the twelfth of the radix, inimical to the MC because it occupies the sign Leo, coming by direction and transit to that same MC, badly disposed in the radix and at the time of the direction and the transit. And the same reasoning applies to the other things signified.

10. If two Planets [that are] the same or related in signification, either by analogy, such as the Sun and Jupiter for honors, [or] Saturn and Mars for illnesses, or by signification from their radical determination, or by both, should transit at the same time by body or by concordant aspect through the same place of the same or related signification (as above), then their signification and virtue for the effect will be doubled, and consequently the magnitude of that effect. But the conjunction of those transiting in that place is stronger than their aspects; especially if it is a conjunction of the lights or of one of them with another of the Planets. And this aphorism is plain from many experiences. And therefore, the conjunction of the Sun and the Moon in the degrees of the malefics in the natal figure or in their opposite [degrees] must be carefully noted, especially when both of the lights or one of them rules the first [house]; but a malefic in whose degree there is a conjunction is a significator of illnesses or death, or it is inimical to the ASC. For such conjunctions certainly signify illnesses or death when [accompanied] by a concordant direction; and the effect begins on the very day of the conjunction as I have often experienced it. Similarly, the conjunction of the rulers of the ASC [and] the eighth of the radix in the eighth of the radix, and especially in the place of a Planet in the eighth with a lethal direction, is lethal at the time of that conjunction. And in short, the conjunction of two or more Planets over the place of another Planet must be very carefully noted; and it must be seen what these Planets are determined to, so that a correct judgment of that event may be made; and these [considerations] can be applied similarly to conjunctions made in the

places of good or evil aspects.

11. The transits of two Planets related in their signification, as [mentioned] above, occurring at the same time through different places, with the Planets themselves mutually related by nature or by radical signification (in the same way as the places of the ruler of the MC and the ruler of the second house, are said to be of a mutually related signification; and the places of the ruler of the twelfth and the ruler of the eighth), strengthen themselves in turn for a more violent effect. For two concordant transits are stronger than one.

12. If there is a cluster of Planets in a particular house, a Planet transiting through that cluster acts in accordance with its own nature and the nature and determination of each Planet, when it will transit through their individual places; and from the succession[63] of transits, the succession of producing an accident will be discovered, or what other accidents will accompany it.

13. The lights coupled to a transiting Planet by body or by a concordant aspect, even if they are alien to its analogous or radical signification, do nevertheless increase the force of the transit. How much more then will they increase [it] with a related signification?

14. One should take note of the status of the radical places through which there are transits in revolutions. For if the radical place of Saturn is in the eighth, and Saturn is in the twelfth of a revolution, especially [when it is] badly disposed and badly configured in its own radical place, on the day on which the ruler of the ASC will transit through that same radical place, either an illness or a danger to the life will occur; but especially, if at the time of the transit, Mars or Saturn or either of the lights should badly aspect that place. And not only should one pay attention to the state of the place through which the transit is made, but also [that] of the transiting Planet itself. For if Mars, transiting through the ASC of

---

[63] Reading *successio* 'succession' rather than *successus* 'success' or 'result'.

the radix, is in the eighth or twelfth of the revolution and also badly disposed, its transit through the ASC will be very bad.

15. The transit of planets that are conjoined through the degree of a direction of the radix, even an empty [degree]—that is, one that is not the place of a radical Planet or cusp—is not without an effect, indeed there will be a notable effect if that transit is of the conjunction of the lights, and especially with an eclipse.

16. The actual virtue of a transit of the Moon lasts through 6 hours before and after the partile transit, but in the case of the other Planets, for one day before and after, by the common agreement of Astrologers that esteems partile aspects much more than platic. And yet whenever a Planet by its own orb of virtue covers the place through which a transit is said to be made, it has a force efficacious to produce the effect of the Planet, especially the swifter planets, such as the Moon, which effect is often produced quicker or slower than the limits given above, because a single transit unequal by itself to [producing] an effect, would demand the necessary concourse of other causes also influencing the act, which occurs either quicker or slower. And it must be noted that the future effect depends upon a transit, not only with regard to its actual time, but also with regard to its own nature, mode, and circumstances; for a transit produces all these things; and consequently they can also be foreseen from a transit. Moreover, when a bad transit [is in effect, and] another bad one follows immediately through the same place in a short interval of time, during a concordant radical direction and revolution of the Sun, as for example if the transit of Saturn, ruler of the 12th, through the ASC is succeeded by the transit of Mars, ruler of the eighth, through that same ASC by body or by square or opposition, it will be lethal. And you will judge similarly about the rest of the significations.

17. If a benefic Planet is in the MC of the radix or is its ruler, and, in a concordant radical direction or revolution of the Sun, or of the Moon [indicative] for honors, that same benefic transits the ASC of the radix or the place of its ruler, especially [if it is] well

disposed and powerfully configured with the ruler of the ASC by syzygy, then good fortune will occur for the Native in dignities or undertakings.

Chapter 14.
How, from What has been Explained so far, Events of the Future can be Predicted by the Stars with Regard to the Kind [of Event], the Year, the Day, and the Hour.

In this chapter we shall repeat in just a very brief compendium what was said about this matter in Books 22, 23, and 24.

First, therefore, there must be available the figure of the nativity exactly rectified, with the true places of the Planets, but especially [those] of the Sun and the Moon.

2. From Book 22, Section 1, Chapter 9; Section 2, Chapter 3; and Section 3, Chapters 3 & 4, the year of the completed direction of each significator to any promissor may be found.

3. From Section 4, Chapters 2 & 3 of that same Book, the kind of future accident signified by any direction may be deduced.

4. From [the instructions in] Book 23, Chapters 4 & 5, the figure of the revolution of the Sun may be erected for the year found above. Then, from Chapter 12, there may be determined from the agreement or disagreement of the radical figure, the direction, and the annual revolution of the Sun, whether or not from those three any effect may be expected in that year, especially one of the kind discovered above.

5. Having made the hypothesis that an effect may be expected, and [one] of the kind as discovered above, let there be made in the annual revolution directions of the concordant significators, from [the instructions in] Book 23, Chapter 15, both to the places in that revolution, and especially to those of the radix

concordant with the signified effect; and from these it will be plain on which days of the year that effect may probably be expected.

6. From [the instructions in] Book 23, Chapter 9, let there be erected the revolutions of the Moon immediately preceding the times indicated by the concordant directions in the revolution of the Sun. And if one of these revolutions closely agrees with the signified effect, let there be established in it, in accordance with [the instructions in] Chapter 15, the directions of concordant significators to concordant promissors, but especially to concordant places in the radix. And in fact, those times of the directions in both revolutions may coincide down to the last day; [and] they promise that the effect [will occur] on that day. And a direction in the revolution of the Moon will also indicate the hour, as can be seen in Book 23, Chapter 16, for events whose hour is given. And [this will be] more certain, the more directions concordant with the effect in both revolutions agree on the same time.

7. But if at that same time concordant transits of the Planets are also made, from [the information in] Chapters 5, 7, 8 & 9 of this Book, there can scarcely be any doubt about the effect signified on the indicated day; and furthermore, the hour [of the effect] can be discovered from the transits and the situation of the Planets with respect to the horizon from [as is explained in] Chapter 11. And this procedure for predicting future events is the most natural [and] genuine of all, and the most certain.

But perhaps the following procedure will seem briefer and more pleasing to some. If a revolution of the Sun agrees with a radical direction, it may be looked at in the ephemerides what sort of day it is for the individual days of the revolutions of the Moon, and what the celestial state of the Planets is [when] compared to the radical figure and the radical direction. And on the day on which that state is perceived to be more concordant with that direction, let the figure of the revolution of the Moon be erected. For if the times of the concordant directions in both the revolutions of the Sun and the Moon agree down to the day, [the effect] will be on [that] day and hour, as the statement was made above.

You will object: this procedure for discovering the state of the whole year and the true time of events is not only very drawn out, but also overrun with confusion. For besides the radical directions, there are also directions of the revolutions that have to be determined, both of the annual and also the monthly revolutions, and of the angles as well as of the individual Planets—not only through the individual places of the radix, but also through the places of the revolution, scattered through the whole zodiac. Moreover, since there are 10 significators—the ASC, the MC, the Part of Fortune, and the 7 Planets, and among these there are 4 principal aspects, the opposition, trine, square, [and] sextile, of which the trine, square, and sextile are duplicated on the right (dexter) and the left (sinister). Therefore, every significator in a revolution can be directed to 56 places [counting] only the aspects of the Planets in a single figure; consequently, for the 10 significators in it there are 560 directions made, just to the aspects of the Planets; to which, if there are added the 63 directions of those 10 significators to the bodies of the Planets, [their number] rises up to 623 directions to be determined in a single figure, such as a revolution of the Sun. And since the directions of a revolution of the Sun should be determined for those same significators both for the places of the radix as well as for [those of] the revolution of the Sun, the 623 must therefore be doubled, making 1246 directions to be calculated for a [single] revolution of the Sun. Therefore, in each revolution of the Moon, both because of itself and because of the revolution of the Sun and [the consideration of] the radical figure, 1869 directions are generated; and consequently, for 12 revolutions of the Moon in a year 22,428 directions[64] are generated; to which 1246 [more] must be added for the Sun, making for the whole year at least 23,674[65] directions for the revolutions of the Sun and the Moon, to be determined down to the day, and also to be judged, so that, with the associated transits that are also very numerous, the state of the whole year may become

---

[64] The text has 22,028 by mistake.

[65] The text has 23,2[7]4 by mistake.

80

known. But if from so great and so confusing a task some Demon might be able to extricate himself correctly and scientifically, there is no human who could do it. And consequently, this doctrine is either not true, or it must be confessed that judicial Astrology is incomprehensible by a human, and therefore he ought to abandon it.

But I reply first. A wolf always seems bigger than he actually is; and Astrology is indeed the most difficult of the physical sciences, according to the common [saying], *A thing that is beautiful is difficult*. However, it should not therefore be laid aside by man, but it should rather be pursued more avidly with intelligence.

I reply second. In the old or common Astrology, which admits annual, diurnal, and monthly progressions, then the revolutions of the Sun and the Moon handed down by Cardan, scarcely fewer operations occur if the individual [factors] in a higher sense are to be minutely examined and considered; and if the revolutions are to be separately or absolutely judged without reference to the nativity, as Cardan himself did in his *Book on Revolutions*, especially since he admitted the terms of the Planets.[66]

I reply third. In the case of the revolutions of the Sun and the Moon, not [all of] those aforesaid 10 significators should be directed, but only the principal ones, namely the ASC, the MC, the Sun in the revolutions of the Sun, and the Moon in the revolutions of the Moon. And [even] this is not always necessary, but [only] after it has been perceived from a radical direction falling in some particular year and with a concordant revolution of the Sun, that some new effect that is especially noteworthy for good or evil is to be expected. If the significator of the direction is a cusp, such as the ASC, [then] the ASC of the revolution will also have to be directed. If it is a Planet, that same Planet will have to be directed in

---

[66] Taking the terms into account would at least double the amount of work, for not only would the condition of the ruler of a significator's sign have to be considered, but also the condition of the ruler of the significator's term. Thus, Cardan's procedure would also be more tedious than Morin's, since the latter ignores the terms.

the revolution. But it will always make known much in both the revolutions of the Sun and the Moon to direct the 4 above said significators—the ASC, the MC, the Sun, and the Moon—on account of the Native's great dependence upon them in existing, acting, and experiencing, whether a new direction of the radical [chart] is completed in that year or not. For a year without a new radical direction, is not also one without an action or an experience for the Native. Add [to this] that the previously completed direction of a radical significator to some promissor lasts [in time] until its meeting with another promissor, unless the latter differs from the former by more degrees. Moreover, it will also make known the Planet to direct either in a revolution of the Sun or of the Moon; for indeed it is the one that in that revolution is allotted a determination concordant with what was signified by the radical direction. So that, if an illness or dignity is signified, it will make it known to direct a Planet that is found in the revolution in the 12th house or the 10th, especially if it was also in the 12th or the 10th of the radix, or if it was the ruler of that house. Besides, the significator that will be directed in revolutions for an accident only signified by the nativity, or even by a new or recently elapsed radical direction, should not be directed to all the places of the nativity or the revolution, but only to those, that is to those promissors, which, from their own nature and determination in the nativity or in the revolution, will be more powerful and more concordant to produce that same accident, whether good or evil. And provided that on those days that are indicated by those same directions in the years and months, concordant transits occur, the effects will burst forth on those very days. An astrologer skilled in the concordance of causes and effects, will only need a few directions to [know] the state of the whole year, that is to recognize the Native's principal changes emanating from the stars in that year.

But since it is certain that effects will never happen, at least from [the action of] the stars without the actual concourse of concordant transits, or at least [perhaps] very rarely from syzygies, as was explained in Chapter 12, it will be briefer to note down from the ephemerides the transits of the Planets through the places of the nativity—those [transits] that are more concordant with the accident signified, whether good or evil. Then to consider whether any concordant direction of the revolution of the Sun may fall upon one of the days indicated by the transits; and this without conjecturing, from the comparison of the distance of the promissor from the significator, with the distance of the indicated day from the first day of the revolution, before the matter is defined by calculation; and by not taking in a revolution of the Sun a significator and a promissor distant by 300 degrees[67] for a transit that is made on the 60th day from the beginning of the revolution of the Sun. Having assumed this, if also in a revolution of the Moon, closely preceding the same day as the transit, any concordant direction falls at that same time, then there will be no doubt about [the occurrence of] the effect. And this is a secret of the science, evident nevertheless in the figures shown in this book and in Book 23, by means of which a confident and sagacious Astrologer can advance by the right path through the densest forest of directions surrounding the object [of interest].

But lest tyros be deterred in this new doctrine from the search for the so much desired truth, we shall set forth here for their benefit two of the above said procedures in a systematic method.

First. Direct the principal significators of the annual revolution—the ASC, the MC, the Sun, the Moon, and the Planet whose noteworthy radical direction is completed in that year, then their rulers if it seems to be needful; and dispose the arcs of the individual directions according to the order of their ascensions in the first column of a Table made for that year, which is properly called a *speculum* for that year.

Second. See on what numbered day from the beginning of the annual revolution each month begins and at what hour, or what is the distance in time from the beginning of the [annual] revolution

---

[67] Reading *300* for *;00* in the Latin text.

to the beginning of each month. And having put the names of the months with that many days and hours cross from the above said arcs with the approximate same number [of days], as the number [of days] for each month, in the second column of that same Table; and so it will then be plain which directions of the year fall in the individual months.

Third. Having erected the revolutions for the whole year, arrange their times similarly in the third column of the above said Table, that is the month, day, and hour of the beginning of the revolution; and thus it will similarly be plain which directions of the year fall in the individual revolutions of the Moon.

Fourth. Having prepared this, each annual direction of a particular significator that is concordant with a radical direction may be taken, that is, its arc may be taken from the first column of the Table and it may be reduced to time by the first and second Table of Directions for revolutions of the Sun[68] [given in] Book 23, Chapter 15 (unless you would prefer from the beginning [of the listing] to reduce the arcs of the individual annual directions immediately to days, hours, and minutes of the annual revolution, which individual times arranged in order will be understood to have been [measured] from the beginning of the annual revolution). And if the number of the time is the same as the number of the beginning of any month, that direction will fall at the beginning of that month; [but] if it is different, subtract from it the nearest smaller number of the beginning of a month, taken from the second column; and there will remain the number of days and hour of that month in which that annual direction will be completed.

Fifth. From the time found, subtract the nearest time of the be-

---

[68] These tables are on p. 653 of the *Astrologia Gallica* and are constructed by setting 360 degrees of arc equal to 365.25 days. The reader with a pocket calculator can turn arc into days by multiplying arc by 1.014583, and days into arc by dividing days by that same constant (or by multiplying days by 0.9856263). (The fundameatal equation should be 360 degrees = 365.2422 days, but the difference is slight.)

ginning oa a revolution of the Moon [as given] in the third column, and there will remain the difference of the two times, which, from the Second and Third Table for the revolutions of the Moon,[69] will give the arc of the equator, which, added to the right or oblique ascension of the MC or the ASC, or to the Sun or Moon in the figure of the revolution of the Moon, will show in the "Tables of Ascensions" of Regiomontanus[70] where the monthly direction of either one of those significators extends to. If, therefore, a direction concordant with the annual direction is then completed, and then there is also made a concordant transit of the Planets, the effect signified by the radical direction will happen at that time or [on that very] day; which, however, can also happen from a transit concordant with a single direction of a concordant annual or monthly revolution—indeed, [it can happen] from a transit alone with a radical direction and a concordant revolution of the Sun or the Moon, especially if the transit is a noteworthy and strong. But the more causes concur, the more certainly and efficaciously the effect is produced. The same thing may be done, if you like, for the individual annual directions, whether a new radical direction is completed in the same year or not. And so the state of the year will be made perfectly plain, if the right judgment is made about the individual [directions].

Another and briefer such procedure is [possible] without [the use of the preceding table. Having taken from the ephemerides the day of a transit that agrees with the signification of an effective radical direction, that is, with the radical signification of a concordant nativity, count the number of days completed of the time from

---

[69] These tables are on p. 657 of the *Astrologia Gallica* and are constructed by setting 360 degrees of arc equal to 27.325 days. The reader with a pocket calculator can turn this arc into days by multiplying the arc by 0.0759028, and days into arc by dividing the days by that same constant (or by multiplying the days by 13.17475.) (The fundamental equation should be 360 degrees = 27.32158 days, but the difference is slight.)

[70] These tables were included in Regiomontanus's *Tabulae directionum profectionumque...* [Tables of Directions and Profections...Very Useful in Nativities] (Augsburg: Erhard Ratdolt, 1490). Often reprinted.

the beginning of the annual revolution to that same day, and turn that into degrees of the equator by means of the Second and Third Table of Directions for revolutions of the Sun, and add that arc to the right or oblique ascension of the concordant significator, chosen in the figure of the revolution of the Sun, and find the sum in the tables of right or oblique ascension, and it will then be plain whether that significator extends to a concordant promissor in the nativity or in the revolution of the Sun. For if that is the case, there is a great probablity of a future effect on that very day. But for greater certainty, reckon the time similarly from the beginning of the monthly revolution most nearly preceding the day found above down to that same day, and turn that into degrees of the equator with the Second and Third Tables of directions for the revolutions of the Moon. And add that arc to the right or oblique ascension of the concordant significator, chosen in the figure of the revolution of the Moon, and find the sum in the Tables of Ascensions as before, and it will then also be plain whether that significator extends to a concordant promissor in the nativity or in the revolution of the Moon. And if this is the case, there is the greatest probablity of a future effect on that very day.

But if there are many days on which transits take place thus, the judgment will have to be for the stronger one. For even though an effect strongly signified by a radical direction may happen on a single day, not on several days; nevertheless, to hit the goal with the first arrow in this most difficult science is very difficult for the human intellect, but not impossible; and continual exercise in this procedure is required to achieve this, along with an uncommon shrewdness of intellect that is able to discern which of the whole year's transits is more appropriate and powerful to actuate the potential of a radical direction, so that [needless] labor may be reduced.

Besides, I don't think there is any need to caution [the Reader] that if the significators to be directed are situated in the descending half of the *Caelum*,[71] the arcs of the equator about which [we

---

[71] The right side of the chart.

spoke] above will have to be added to the oblique descensions of those significators for their directions; or (which is easier) the place diametrically opposite the significator will have to be directed by its ascensions, and the place diametrically opposite the direction will be obtained; for we suppose that that is sufficiently known from the doctrine of directions.

Therefore, we will only caution [the Reader] that since the doctrine we have set forth up to now for directions, revolutions, and transits is natural and uniform in [both] a nativity and its revolutions and their directions, then it is also true, as was very plainly shown by the examples given in Book 23. This alone will have to be relied upon, and the labor must not be spared for [making] the lunar revolutions for the whole year, especially when a new radical direction of that year is completed, or it is allotted a determination in the radix that is of particular moment. For, it will always disclose the revolutions of the Moon and their directions to consult either for any annual direction or for any concordant transit. And particular events are known from this; and their investigated times can be predicted by an astrologer with great labor, because in fact particular effects not only depend on universal causes but also on particular ones, which must also be taken into account for those particular effects.

You will object second. From the doctrine set forth by us above, the future accidents of the Native cannot be predicted. If indeed the radical figure and its directions do not act without revolutions, both of the Sun and of the Moon, and the transits of the Planets through the places of those 3 figures from what was said above; and those revolutions must be erected for the place in which the Native is located at the time of each revolution, either of the Sun or of the Moon, according to Book 23, Chapters 4 and 9, which places cannot be known in advance from the nativity. On the contrary, it can scarcely be known in advance by [even] one year before the time of any revolution of the Sun; therefore, Astrology is useless and unreliable for predicting future things.

I reply first. The objection is only applicable to those Natives who travel at a distance, not to those who remain in their native place, which are especially women,[72] or who remain near that place.

I reply second. From the nativity and the radical directions it can be known whether the Native is going to travel and at what time; up till then, revolutions erected for the natal place will be useable.

I reply third. Some journeys are long and some are short. Those that do not exceed 50 French leagues[73] from the natal place scarcely make any perceptible change in the influx of revolutions erected for the natal place, unless from that a difference of ASC's is produced that exceeds 2 degrees.[74] But for revolutions beginning with the Native further distant, especially [with the ASC] in a different sign, they must be erected for the place where he is; and thus the future accidents in that year may be known in advance for him. And it must be noted that a revolution of the Sun, erected for the place where the Native is, is valid for that whole year, however far distant he may travel during it, for he carries along with him the influx newly impressed at the beginning of that revolution, no differently than that he carries with him throughout his whole life the influx received at birth just as it was impressed on him. But the

---

[72] In Morin's time, women generally stayed at home and did not travel nearly so much as men

[73] About 125 statute miles, which would be equivalent to some 2.5 degrees of longitude at 45° N.

[74] A French league was about 25 statute miles; hence, 50 leagues would be 125 miles. In the latitude of Paris, a degree of longitude is equal to about 49.6 miles, so in the worst case—when the Native was due east or west of his birthplace at the time of the revolution—the RAMC would be increased or decreased by 2°30' or so. Again in the worst case—with 0 Capricorn on the Midheaven—such a change in the RAMC would alter the longitude of the Ascendant by 5.4°. To keep it down to the 2-degree maximum that Morin mentions, the maximum E or W distance from the birthplace would have to be restricted to 46 miles or 18½ French leagues. But in an average case, this distance would be increased to about 100 miles or 40 French leagues.

revolutions of the Moon will [also] be erected for the place in which the Native will then be. For just as the revolutions of the Sun are related to the nativity that they actuate, so the revolutions of the Moon are related to the revolution of the Sun that they actuate similarly. And hence, Astrology cannot be said to be unusable or unreliable. Especially because the Native can conjecture for individual years, and all the more for individual months, where in fact he will be at the time of the next following revolution of the Sun or of the Moon. But whoever does otherwise and gives an opinion about the Native's individual acts throughout the whole course of his life just from his nativity and its directions, or even with the addition of revolutions erected only for the place of birth, with that Native then far away, will certainly be deceived in many things, and more or less on account of the discrepancy in the revolutional figures [erected] in different places. For the stars do not influence the Native except where he is. But let what has already been said about this suffice.

Chapter 15.
Some Principal Rules of Prudence to be [Observed] by an Astrologer in Bringing Forth a Useful Opinion from the Stars.

Judicial astrology as regards its theory is a wisdom than which nothing in the physical sciences is more sublime, more divine, more worthy of human study, but which in practice requires so much prudence and circumspection with regard to the particular man about whom a judgment is to be made, with regard to the Celestial causes, from which they are derived in essence, to be conserved, to be changed and corrupted, with regard to the place in which [the native] is located, with regard to the persons with whom he happens have some good or evil thing, and with regard to other things that must be combined in divers fashion, so that in making judgments on present or future things, neither Medicine, nor Jurisprudence, nor Political Prudence, deserve to be compared with it.

Therefore, it was not without justice that Cardan said after Book I, Aphorism 25,[75] "It is difficult to judge by those things that have been written, still more difficult to hand down the art itself, and most difficult of all to discover that same art," [and] he rightly concludes, "Therefore, Astrology, as it is the most beautiful [art], is also the most laborious and difficult."

It is not at all surprising then that when judicial [astrology] is practiced by ignorant persons and sycophants, it is very often exposed to the ridicule, especially of the uninformed, stupidly ranting against that which to them is absolutely unknown; since it may also sometimes happen [that] a man very skilled in this science, which has also been set forth purely and truly, can be deceived in his own judgments, either because he has not surveyed exactly or weighed everything pertinent to his judgment, or because, having also considered everything carefully, [his] conclusions are not for an absolute necessity, especially in things that are subordinate to the will. And, as I do not deny that I have several times erred (having been led astray in particular by the old doctrine), thus frankly I am always ready to have detected my errors that have occurred, or that I have departed from the doctrine I have already set forth; still less than equal was my proper trusting in that, or that I had deviated from the rules of prudence that I had [normally] observed in practice. Therefore, lest anyone already properly instructed in the [doctrine of] Astrology that we have set forth should dash against those same boulders, we have stated some important rules of prudence necessary for an Astrologer in judgments that it will be most useful to add here.

First. From the figure of a nativity presented to you whose time is not really well established either by observation of the stars or by rectification by means of the Native's accidents, pronounce nothing with certainty, but only on the hypothesis that the figure is true, and therefore [the judgments are] doubtful. But, having been

---

[75] Jerome Cardan, *Aphorismorum astronomicorum segmenta septem, Opera Omnia*, p. 30.

given the true time of the nativity, it is proper to pronounce with certainty about the Native's body, his inclinations and intelligence, but only probably and conjecturally about his actions and the events of his fortune.

2. When you have been asked to erect and judge the figure of a nativity for any person, inquire in connection with this about the place of his nativity, his sex, his race, whether he has both parents or neither, or of what quality, whether he has brothers or sisters, whether they are prior [to him] by birth or later, whether he has married or has devoted himself to an ecclesiastical life, whether he has children, what is his profession; then, what was his previous status, and what is his present status. For, when you have been made more certain about these things, you may know your subject more perfectly and his disposition with regard to the Celestial influxes and forces for future accidents. For even though you can[76] divine many of those things from the figure alone, nevertheless because so much will be inquired of the astrologer in the future, it is preferable to avoid the labor to seek out the past and present things, for the knowledge of these things is of no small use in [gaining] an idea of future things. And in this conjectural science, bases of certitude must be procured from every source. Add to these that, given the time of a nativity, it must be rectified by past accidents.

3. Accidents [affecting] the body and the mind are much more subject to Celestial causes than are accidents of chance. For this depends both on the Native's own will and on the will and power of another, then on laws and on other arrangements of inferior fate. And consequently, in an accident of chance strongly signified also by the radix, by a direction, and by a revolution, see what the Native's status is; for if he was free and a law unto himself, he will be extrinsically capable [of experiencing] any kind of accident of chance, either good, or evil, but if indeed he was an exile, in prison, cloistered, a servant, sick, [or] powerless, then the accidents of chance that are incompatible with such a status are impeded, for so

---

[76] Reading *possis* rather than *pessis*.

long as that status or its cause lasts. But, with this taken away, also without a direction, a change of fortune may occur. And so, those who were oppressed by the tyrannical power of Cardinal Richelieu and were sent into exile or into prison, by his death alone obtained the end of his oppression, and they recovered their former honors. But the servants of that same Cardinal lost their own honors in his court. Wherefore, in predicting, the reason for the cause of the good luck or bad luck for individuals must be taken into account, otherwise an error can occur if the prognosis is only made from the figure [made for] the Native.

4. Love and hate disturb the mind and the judgment of the Astrologer in [making] his predictions, lest he should look at [several] individual things and judge [them] impartially to be equal; [when in fact] they act to lessen the maximum [effect] and somewhat augment the minimum [effect]. And so, the Astrologer should concern himself solely with the love of truth, for then his mind is more perfectly disposed to receiving and expounding that divine motion and light that is required in [making] prophecies.

5. The counsel or judgment of an Astrologer is much more certain in relation to present things, such as illness, ambition for [higher] rank, a contract of marriage, a lawsuit, , etc., than in relation to future things; for in both the latter and the former he sees the state of the Celestial causes equally well, but in present things he sees the [immediate] situation of the Native and of his inferior fate, which he does not see in future things, except perhaps by an obscure conjecture.

6. A particular fate and a particular cause submits to a universal cause because of that law of nature, by which the stronger overcomes the weaker; consequently, many in the same ship are drowned together, and many are slain in the same battle, [who are] not exposed to these misfortunes by their own nativities or [which occur] without an appropriate direction or a revolution. For who will have said that all those in the same ship who were drowned at the same hour have charts, directions, and revolutions for that

same kind of death and at that same time? But perhaps if not all the causes are present, there are some, a chart for this [person], a direction for that one, a revolution for another, and a transit for still another, and that is a sufficient [cause] in a common or public danger; which consequently he ought much more to guard against— [namely] which one of the many causes occurring at the same time will be the one harmful to himself; but it scarcely seems likely that of the 100 men perishing by shipwreck at the same time in the same ship, no one by his own chart is immune to submersion at that very hour. Therefore, they are perishing from the malign fate of sailors or of the army of the commander to whom they are subject; but these are universal causes [inherent in] sailing and battle.

7. From only the chart of a [single] native, you should never assert anything strongly (at least with any certainty) about an accident common to him and to another person, such as a lawsuit, a peace agreement, friendship, marriage, etc., nor about accidents pertaining to other persons, such as his parents, brothers, spouse, children, servants, a friend, [or] an enemy, unless you have inspected the natal figures of those persons. For common accidents depend upon a common fate and one appropriate to the other person, more so than [simply] to himself. Wherefore, you may confide sensibly in figures extracted from the Native's figure for other persons, as we have stated in Book 22, Section 4, Chapter 6, although these also have a close and extraordinary sympathy with the Native, as is shown there.

8. When you are going to judge about whatever kind of accident, such as [one involving] ability, habits, riches, honors, etc., inspect the house of the figure to which those accidents belong, namely the first for ability and habits, the second for riches, etc., and also those that are associated in the signification, which are the 2nd and the 10th for riches and honors, the 8th and the 12th for illness and death, and also their opposite [houses]. And judge about those accidents from the signs and Planets occupying those houses by body or by rulership, then also by strong aspect; and also from the nature of a Planet analogous to the accident, having [also]

looked at the celestial and terrestrial state of the Planets as well as the Native's social status and his profession.

9. Before you render judgment about any sort of future accident [occurring] either to an old man or to a youth, see whether the Native is going to live up to a time concordant with that accident by directions and by his age. For if life is lacking, the other things [that appear to be] signified, such as dignities, marriage, children, etc., will be impossible, however strongly they may be signified in the nativity. And in this respect, many Astrologers of a great name have very often been deceived, either from inattention or because they had not recognized the true *anaereta* or destroyer of life, which should be determined not only by directions of the significators of life, but especially by concurrent revolutions concordant with the Sun and the Moon and also with their directions, in an exactly rectified figure of the nativity.

10. Take care in judgments and predictions, lest you descend to a particular accident, especially [when judging] from the Native's figure alone, but go no farther than the kind or type of accident, as we have said in Book 21, Section 4, Chapters 2 & 3.

11. At the first glance, you may [confidently] say that it is an unfortunate nativity in which Saturn or Mars or both of them are in the same degree with the Sun & the Moon, or one of these is besieged by them, or individual malefics are joined to the lights, or when the Moon is under the Sun beams, or it is conjoined to Mars or opposed or squared [by it], or when all the Planets are in the 6th, 8th, or 12th, or when Saturn & Mars are in the angles while the Sun and the Moon are in cadent [houses], or, when the Sun and the Moon are cadent, other Planets are retrograde, or when the Sun, the Moon, Jupiter & Venus are all impeded. Wherefore, in such nativities you must beware lest you rashly promise good things.

12. The Sun in the 1st, 10th, and 9th customarily confers great glory and exceptional honors unless there is a great contrariety elsewhere [in the chart]. When, therefore, you have seen it in those

houses, do not rush to judgment, but pay attention to its Celestial state and that of the ruler of the ASC, and if nothing opposes, predict outstanding things.

13. If you see three Planets in the fiery Triplicity and especially [if one of them is] the Sun, along with any of the superior Planets, you can predict great glory and power for the Native if their determination is in agreement, especially if his lineage is suitable [for such things]. But if you have found Mercury in the airy Triplicity with three other Planets, you can safely promise sublimity of talent.

14. Many Planets in the same house, especially with the Sun or the Moon or with both, always presages something extraordinary in excess according to the essential significations of that house, as has happened to me.[77]

15. The more distinguished and heroic nativities are not just from the influx of the benefics, but they are also mingled with the strong influxes of the malefics, whence occur lawsuits, wars, then victories, by which the nativities are rendered more illustrious.

16. Nativities in which the degree of a closely preceding great conjunction[78] is in the ASC or in the MC, or is occupied by the Sun or the Moon or the ruler[79] of the ASC or the MC, presage the distinguished sublimity of the Native if other things [in the chart] are in agreement, especially if that conjunction is made with the mutation of Triplicity.

17. The greatest prudence is required in predicting the Native's profession. for it depends on either the will of his parents or on the Native's own talents, or also on the laws and customs of his native land—as in China, where without royal consent it is not permitted for children to desert their father's profession. Besides, in

---

[77] Morin had four planets in the twelfth house.

[78] He means a conjunction of Jupiter and Saturn.

[79] Reading *domino* 'ruler' father than *dominio* 'rulership'.

France where commerce is the foulest of all dignities, the Nobles are accustomed to destine their children to arms and also sometimes to the Church, only rarely to the Senate because of the immense cost of those dignities. But the Senators commonly destine their children to the Senate on account of bribes and hereditary succession, frequently to the Church on account of licit dealings, more rarely to arms. But the middle class and men of the lowest rank are not content with their own lot, except for the more simple-minded ones, but the stronger they are in mind or talent, or the more powerful in wealth, the more they court for success in arms, in the Senate, in the Church, in the treasury, according to what talent is preponderant in each one. And so, the profession should not always be declared from Planets in the 10th or from its rulers, but the scheme of the significators of talent and customs must also be especially considered, that is the Planets in the first or its rulers, especially if they were with the lights or the ruler of the 10th, for they often determine natives to a [particular] profession like unto their own nature. And not only do they select a profession for the Native concordant with their own talent, but those parents are also careful to observe very closely the talent of the children, so that they may make them fortunate with a suitable profession. Therefore, in predicting the profession, there must be no little consideration of the [Native's] talent, about which the Old [Astrologers] have said nothing at all. And since the bodily constitution and the facial appearance are also due to the impression of the stars, something indeed little will come forth from that character to make known a conjecture of the profession with greater certainty, for military men and ecclesiastics, but especially monks and nuns, as very often they are distinguished by an appearance concordant with their own profession.

18. When the Native and those around him are disposed concordantly in inferior fate to some future effect, more can be produced from a weak celestial cause than from a strong cause, when the Native is not disposed as above or is striving against it. And so, in an intemperate youth, addicted to violent activities, in summer,

and in war, a weak direction causing illness, can stir up a great and dangerous illness, which a stronger direction will not stir up in an intemperate elder person and one prudently taken precaution for himself. But in an intemperate elder person and one exposed to death, if any sort of direction causing illness occurs with a similar revolution, do not promise [a continuation of] life or escape [from illness], especially if he may be be treated by unskilled physicians. For they emulate all the arts of Mercury before the rest, and they deliver to Charon the souls of men expelled from their bodies by [the physicians'] ignorance of medicine.[80]

19. In [making] a general judgment of a natal figure, the scheme of the directions must be taken into account—whether they agree and in a suitable age. But much more in the judgment of directions, the scheme of the natal figure must be taken into account—whether it agrees with those directions; namely, because a direction without the agreement of the nativity can accomplish nothing, as we have said elsewhere.

20. In any accident that is also strongly signified in the nativity, pay close attention in the figure to the causes contrary to it. As for example, if luxury is signified, pay attention to the celestial causes analogous to chastity; and see whether they are determined in the first [house] to habits by their location and rulership, or by connection with Planets in the first, or by rulership of the first; and weigh both causes, and judge for the stronger with moderation. And do the same for whatever other kinds of accidents, in the radix as well as in directions and revolutions.

21. The greatest prudence of this art that must be held to be a secret: it is, to pronounce boldly about things that are evidently and strongly signified by the celestial indications and without any strong contrariety, unless for the thing signified there is in inferior fate some huge fixed impediment, such as priesthood with respect

---

[80] Morin disagreed with some of the common practices of his fellow physicians, such as the bleeding of patients.

to matrimony or military dignity (even though in my own time I have seen Cardinals, Archbishops, Bishops, and Abbots—for shame!—also distinguished in military dignities in wars against [fellow] Catholics), or by castration with respect to the begetting of offspring, and such like. But to predict only doubtfully about things that are signified obscurely, weakly, or with notably contrariety, or with a meager difference of contrarieties, and to explain the contrarieties, probably nevertheless by concluding for the stronger part because of its prominence.

22. When the causes are mutually contradictory for any accident, such as for death, whether it is for a future natural death or for a violent one; for a dignity, whether it is for a future military or ecclesiastical one, and such like, pay attention to the strength of the contrary causes; and do not base your conclusion on only one if the causes are equally strong, as if they were in equilibrium. But conclude for both of them in succession, or for a mixture of them. Just as in the death of Cardinal Richelieu, which was partly a violent one because of the iron that was often applied,[81] and partly natural, from an unexpected fever, by which he was finally killed; the contrariety of which [arose] from Jupiter in the eighth, but in exile and with a violent fixed star in square with the lights. And thus many persons are moved forward in childhood to ecclesiastical dignities by their parents who are magnates, [but] who then, excited by the stimulus of their own nature, having dismissed those dignities, marry, and strive for judicial or military [dignities]. But where one part is very weak, conclude only for the other.

23. In the prediction of a future accident, much more attention must be paid to the celestial causes than to the *present* status of the Native, and it must be judged according to them. For it cannot be known (unless perhaps by a very uncertain conjecture) what sort of status the Native will have then; moreover, the celestial causes of that same future accident may be seen, which dispose the Native and those around him in inferior fate to the future accident by their

---

[81] This is a reference to the surgery that was performed on the Cardinal.

own virtue. But whoever has done otherwise, will without doubt be deceived many times.

24. Take care that you do not ever determine the precise time of an accident from the radix, to be signified [solely] by a radical direction and an annual revolution, without first considering the annual and monthly directions, for it is from these [that you can] determine the precise time; and without considering these, the transits of the Planets, even concordant ones, often fail, but very seldom with these.

25. For acquiring notable fame, and for raising on high the glory of Astrology, you should have many selected nativities [in your collection]; not only [those] of middle-class and working-class men, but especially of kings, princes, and magnates of both sexes exactly erected and rectified. Then, when from a radical figure, a radical direction, and a revolution of the Sun, you perceive an important good or evil to be strongly signified, according to the doctrine that we have set forth, without any contrariety that is of any importance, that very good or evil may boldly be predicted for that year; either for one person only, whose figure is available, or also for many others, especially courtiers, if the danger is absent.[82] Indeed, why not [find] the very day of the accident, investigated and determined from [the instructions in] Chapter 14, for the greater glory. And you should not overlook such opportunities but rather you should diligently watch for them. I was able to do this very often and very easily, and yet [sometimes] I didn't do it, because, busied with other tasks, I did not take advantage of those opportunities; and then, the opportunity having gone away, I was often sorry, not so much because profit would come from it, but because glory and praise of Astrology would come from it. But, having considered it more carefully, it seemed to me that this

---

[82] The Latin has *si periculum absit* 'if the danger is absent (or distant)', or 'if there is no danger'. I am uncertain what Morin meant by these words. We could read *adsit* instead of *absit*, and then it could be translated 'if the danger is there (or present)'.

had not happened without divine providence. For if I had been present, and it was unquestionably as I had predicted, especially about magnates of the court; not only would a more illustrious fame have resulted, but over and above that I would have been overwhelmed at Paris by commands and entreaties for erecting and judging figures, so that I would never have been able to bring this work to completion, which, so that I might finally complete it and make it known to the public for the glory of GOD, I have very often declined any particular gain from the practice of Astrology, even from many magnates of both sexes, on account of the lack of time. But from the science already plainly set forth, a learned astrologer who follows my counsel in this part will frequently experience its outstanding utility with joy.

26. If Saturn is in exile in the 9th in the mobile sign Cancer and is conjoined to the Part of Fortune in the natal figure, portending misfortune and disgrace in lengthy travels or outside his homeland, certainly that will happen at some time unless the Native diligently guards himself; therefore, it is right for him to know that he is prone to such misfortune. And the misfortune will happen principally through revolutions, in accordance with the nature of the house that Saturn is in. The Most Serene Prince Lord Condé[83] had such a radical constitution. Through many years he was always the victor and fortunate in war; but in his revolution of the year 1646, having a direction of the radical MC to the square of Mars, and Saturn on the cusp of the seventh [house] of the annual revolution, retrograde in Taurus, a terrestrial sign, and square to the MC of the radix, he set out for Spain in the year 1647, and while besieging Lerida, he was forced to abandon the siege, notwithstanding the trine of the Sun to Saturn, and Jupiter and Venus in the ninth of the revolution; and so it caused [him] misfortune in foreign wars, although from that same revolution he was very fortunate in the year 1646 in his siege of the city of Dunkerque in Flanders. Therefore, the significations of good and evil must be combined in these and

---

[83] Louis II of Bourbon, Prince of Condé (1621-1686), the "Great Condé," a famous and nearly always successful military commander, as Morin says.

100

not judged solely in accordance with one part.

27. Last and first, and therefore the greatest prudence of all, is for an Astrologer to have remembered [that] prediction is a work of future things, than which nothing in Nature is more divine, and to search with his mind united to God and open with prayers that He illuminate his mind for distinguishing [the facts] with truth. For a mind sunk in passions and sins is blind, [and] so unsuited for this wisdom, so that even a learned Astrologer may be deceived in the easier judgments, and may often be made ridiculous; what, therefore, will he do in more difficult and obscure ones, in which many [mutually-] contradictory things are signified to him?

End of the Twenty-fourth Book.

APPENDIX 1

The time used in all of the charts in Book 24 is Local Apparent Time (LAT). To assist the reader who may want to recalculate some of the charts, I have prepared a table of the Equation of Time for the year 1625. That year is approximately in the middle of the time period spanned by the charts. The Equation of Time changes slowly from year to year, but the table shown below is sufficiently accurate for dates within 75 years or more before or after 1625.

The argument of the table is the true longitude of the Sun. To find the value of the Equation of Time locate the solar longitude that is just before the longitude of the Sun and the one just after; these are at 5 degree intervals. Interpolate these two values to get the value for an intermediate longitude. Once found, the Equation of Time can be rounded off to the nearest whole minute.

Table of the Equation of Time for the Year 1625

Sun	Eq.T	Sun	Eq.T	Sun	Eq.T	Sun	Eq.T
0	+7.7	90	+0.9	180	-7.7	270	-0.9
5	+6.1	95	+2.0	185	-9.4	275	+1.6
10	+4.5	100	+3.0	190	-11.0	280	+4.0
15	+2.9	105	+4.0	195	-12.4	285	+6.3
20	+1.4	110	+4.8	200	-13.7	290	+8.4
25	-0.0	115	+5.3	205	-14.7	295	+10.2
30	-1.3	120	+5.6	210	-15.4	300	+11.8
35	-2.3	125	+5.7	215	-15.9	305	+13.1
40	-3.2	130	+5.5	220	-16.1	310	+14.1
45	-3.8	135	+5.0	225	-15.9	315	+14.7
50	-4.2	140	+4.3	230	-15.4	320	+15.0
55	-4.3	145	+3.3	235	-14.5	325	+14.9
60	-4.1	150	+2.1	240	-13.3	330	+14.6
65	-3.7	155	+0.7	245	-11.8	335	+13.9
70	-3.1	160	-0.8	250	-10.0	340	+13.0
75	-2.3	165	-2.5	255	-7.9	345	+11.9
80	-1.3	170	-4.2	260	-5.7	350	+10.6
85	-0.2	175	-5.9	265	-3.3	355	+9.2
90	+0.9	180	-7.7	270	-0.9	360	+7.7

```
LMT = LAT + Equation of Time
LAT = LMT - Equation of time
```

Suppose for example that the Sun in a chart is in 23°19′ of

Scorpio. This is equivalent to 233°19′ or 233.3° to the nearest tenth of a degree. Looking in the table, we find for 230° that the Equation of Time has the value -15.4, and for 235° the value is -14.5. The difference is 0.9 and it is decreasing. We want 3.3/5 or 0.67 of that difference; it will be 0.67 X 0.9 or 0.6., so we subtract that amount from the figure for 230°, and we have -15.4 reduced by 0.6 or -14.8. That is the value in minutes and tenths of a minute. We can round it off, and we will say that the approximate value of the Equation of Time is 15 minutes. Then, if the stated time was 6:05 AM LAT, the equivalent LMT will be 6:05 AM -0:15 or 5:50 AM LMT.

Index of Persons

Abbots, 98
Alchabitius, *astrologer*, 28 n.34
Alexander I, Duke of Florence, 13 n.19
Arabian Astrologers, vii,26 n.33
Archbishops, 98
Asclation, *astrologer*, 3 n.6
Ascletarion, (*see* Asclation)
Astronomers, 36
Balbillus, Tiberius Claudius, *astrologer*, 3 n.6
Bishops, 98
Caesar, Gaius Julius, *general and dictator*, 36
Caligula, Emperor, 3
Campanus of Novara, *mathematician*, 28 n.34
Cardan, Jerome, 1-18,4 n.11,5 n.12,8 n.14,13 n.19,14 n.21,15 n.22, 28 n.34,81 n.66,90
Cardinals, 98
Catholics, 98
Ceresara, Paris, *astrologer*, 4
Chaldeans, 4 n.8,10
Charles V, Emperor, 46
Charon, *mythological figure*, 97
Cicero, Marcus Tullius, *orator, statesman, and literatus*, xi
Clement VII, Pope, 13 n.19
Commissioners, 56
Condé, Louis II of Bourbon, Prince of, *general*, 100
Condren, Charles de, *theologian*, 52,63,64
Courtiers, 99
Cramer, Frederick H., *scholar*, 3 n.6
Deacons, 52
Demon, 81
Devil, 41
Domitian, Emperor, 3

Ecclesiastics, 96
Egyptians, 4,10
Elder persons, 97
Farnese, Alessandro, Cardinal (*see* Paul III)
Fortune-teller, *unidentified*, 68
Francesco Maria of Ferrara, *astrologer*, 4
Gaurico, Luca, Bishop, *astrologer*, 13 n.19
Giuntini, Francesco, *astrologer*, 7
God, 12,30,44,48,66,68,73,100,101
Good Angel, 68
Gustavus Adolphus, King of Sweden, 36,49,61
Henry IV, King of France, 36
Hollandus, John Isaac, *alchemist*, 22
Huguetan, Jean Antoine, *publisher*, 3 n.5
Junctinus (*see* Giuntini, Francesco)
Kepler, John, *astronomer*, 37
Kings, 41,99
Lesdiguières, François de Bonne, Duke of, Constable of France, 50
Lower-class men, 96
Magnates, 99
Menard, Pierre, *publisher*, 28 n.34
Middle-class men, 41,96,99
Military men, 96
Modern Astrologers, vii,48
Monks, 96
Morhard, Ulrich, *publisher*, 18 n.28
Morin, Jean Baptiste, viii-xi,5 n.12,14 n.21,28 n.34,43 n.39,48
n.40,63 n.52,65, 66 n.54,55,67,69,73,95 n.77, 97 n.80
Naibod, Valentine, *astrologer*, viii n.4,25 n.30
Nero, Emperor, 3
Nobles, 96
Nuns, 96
Offusius, Johannes Francus, *physician*, 58
Old Astrologers, 1,2,8,11,20,23,26,48,57,96
Old Chemists, 22

Origanus, David, *mathematician*, 7
Paul III, Pope, 4 n.10
Physicians, 97
Piccinino, Jacopo, *condottiere*, 4 n.9
Pitatus, Petrus, *mathematician*, 18
Placidus di Titus, *astrologer*, viii
Princes, 99
Priests, 52
Ptolemy, Claudius, 1-4,8-12
Rantzau, Henry von, Count, 4 n.9
Ratdolt, Erhard, *publisher*, 85 n.70
Ravaud, Marc Antoine, *publisher*, 3 n.5
Regiomontanus, *astronomer*, 7,85
Richelieu, Armand du Plessis de, Cardinal, 51,56,62,63,92,98
Robson, Vivian, *astrologer*, viii n.4
Robbins, F.E., *editor and translator*, 2 n.3, 4 n.8,8 n.14
Schöner, Johann, *astrologer*, 7
Senators, 96
Simple-minded persons, 96
Stadius, Johann, *mathematician*, 4 n.10
Sub-Deacons, 52
Sulla (*see* Balbillus, Tiberius Claudius)
Superior Astrologers, 1
Thorndike, Lynn, *historian*, 4 n.9-10,18 n.28,58 n.48
Thrasybulus (*see* Thrasyllus, Tiberius Claudius)
Thrasyllus, Tiberius Claudius, *astrologer*, 3 n.6
Tiberius, Emperor, 3
Tronson, Louis, *royal official*, 51,64
Tucci, Tucci, *astrologer*, 4 n.10
Tyard, Pontus de, *poet*, 4 n.10
Villennes, Nicolas de Bourdin, Marquess of, 28 n.34
Woman, *unidentified acquaintance of Morin*, 53,66
Working-class men, 99

BIBLIOGRAPHY

Original Works

Gaurico, Luca
Tractatus astrologicus.
[Astrological Treatise]
Venice: Curtius Troianus Nauó, 1552.

[Green, H.S.]
A Thousand and One Notable Nativities.
London: Modern Astrology, 1915?. 2nd ed. rev.

The Book of Notable Nativities.
Chicago: The Aries Press, 1943. repr. in facs. of the 2nd ed

Holden, James Herschel
A History of Horoscopic Astrology.
Tempe, Az.: A.F.A., Inc., 1996. xv,359 pp. 21 cm. diagrs. tables

Morin, Jean Baptiste
Longitudinum terrestrium nec non coelestium
nova et hactenus optata scientia...
[The New and Hitherto Hoped for Science of
Terrestrial and Celestial Longitudes...]
Paris: J. Libert, 1634. 4to. 164 pp.

Tabulae Rudolphinae ad meridianum Uraniburgi
supputatae a Joanne Baptista Morino, ... ad
accuratum et facile compendium redactae.
[The Rudolphine Tables, Calculated by Jean
Baptiste Morin for the Meridian of Uraniborg, ...
Reduced to an accurate and easy compendium]
Paris: J. Le Brun, 1650. 4to. 117 pp. tables

108

Remarques astrologiques de Jean-Baptiste Morin,
... sur le commentaire du Centiloque de Ptolomée
mise en lumière par Messire Nicolas de Bourdin, ...
[The Astrological Remarks of Jean Baptiste Morin
... on the Commentary on Ptolemy's *Centiloquy*
Published by My Lord Nicolas de Bourdin...]
Paris: P. Ménard, 1657. 4to. 168 pp.

Remarques astrologiques/ de Jean-Baptiste Morin
... sur le Commentaire du Centiloque de Ptolémée
ou la seconde partie de l'Uranie de Messire
Nicolas de Bourdin, marquis de Villennes, etc.
edited by Jacques Halbronn
[with a valuable introduction, notes, and a
bibliography of Morin's works]
Paris: Retz, 1976. repr. of the 1st ed. 303 pp. 20 cm. portr.
facs. tables. biblio.

Astrologia Gallica.
[French Astrology]
The Hague: Adrian Vlacq, 1661. folio. Pref., 784 pp. portr.
diagrs. tables

Regiomontanus
Tabulae directionum profectionumque...
in nativitatibus multum utiles.
[Tables of Directions and Profections...
Very Useful in Nativities]
Augsburg: Erhard Ratdolt, 1490. 4to.

Thorndike, Lynn
A History of Magic and Experimental Science.
New York: Columbia University Press, 1923-1958. 8 vols.

Translations and Commentaries

Morin, Jean Baptiste
*La Théorie des Déterminations Astrologiques
de Morin de Villefranche/conduisant à une
Méthode rationelle pour l'Interprétation du Thême
Astrologique.*
[Morin of Villefranche's Theory of Astrological
Determinations, Leading to a Rational Method for the
Interpretation of the Astrological Chart]
[an abridged translation into French by Henri Selva
(*pseudonym*) of the *Astrologia Gallica*, Book 21]
Paris: Bodin, 1902. vi, 218 pp. 2 plates
Paris: Éditions Traditionelles, 1991. new ed. 224 pp. diagrs.
paper 22 cm.

*The Morinus System of Horoscope Interpretation/
Astrologia Gallica/Book Twenty-One.*
trans. from the Latin by Richard S. Baldwin
Washington: A.F.A., 1974. paper [i-v],109,[1] 23 cm.

Astrologia Gallica/ Book Twenty-Two/Directions.
[with excerpts from Books 2, 13, 15, 17, 18, 20,
23, 24, and Jerome Cardan's works]
trans. from the Latin by James Herschel Holden
Tempe, Az.: A.F.A. Inc., 1994. paper xv,292 pp. diagrs. tables 22 cm.

Astrologia Gallica/ Book Twenty-Three/Revolutions.
trans. from the Latin by James Herschel Holden
Tempe, Az.: A.F.A., Inc., 2003. 1st ed. paper portr. diagrs.
tables 23 cm.
Tempe, Az.: A.F.A., Inc., 2004. 2nd ed. rev. paper portr.
xi,148 pp. diagrs. tables 28 cm.

Astrologia Gallica/Book Eighteen.
[The Strength of the Planets]
trans. from the Latin by Pepita Sanchis Llacer and from her
Spanish version by Anthony Louis LaBruzza
Tempe, Az.: A.F.A., Inc., 2004, paper, 101 pp.

"Jean Baptise Morin's Comments on House Division
in his *Remarques Astrologiques*"
(House Division III)
trans. from the French by James H. Holden
Journal of Research of the AFA 6, Nos. 1&2 (1991):19-35
Tempe, Az.: A.F.A., Inc., 1982-

Suetonius, Gaius Tranquillus
The Lives of the Twelve Caesars.
trans. by Joseph Gavorse
New York: Modern Library, 1931. xvi, 361 pp.

LaVergne, TN USA
23 August 2009
155705LV00002B/14/A